Small Talk

Master the Art of Small Talk Easily and Effectively With These Easy Steps

(Improve Your Social Skills, Stop Anxiety and Develop Your Charisma)

Paul Orosco

Published By **Regina Loviusher**

Paul Orosco

Small Talk: Master the Art of Small Talk Easily and Effectively With These Easy Steps (Improve Your Social Skills, Stop Anxiety and Develop Your Charisma)

ISBN   978-1-998769-67-4

No part of this guidebook shall be reproduced in any form without permission in writing from the publisher except in the case of brief quotations embodied in critical articles or reviews.

Legal & Disclaimer

Table of contents

Chapter 1: What Is The Which Means Of Small Communicate?

You input a smart spot and look for recognized faces. However, you understand that there are not any! Subsequently, have a cross at staying away from the entire condition and desire for a mystery break out.

Sauntering around the table or shifting at some point of the washroom is not a number of the capability ways which you are following to strive not to participate in chatter. In any case, in line with the specialists, there is not anything trivial about the small speak dialogue.

Dominating the compelling artwork of small communicate can help you with attempting no longer to fall into an strange social circumstance, little event, or unique examples where you're an outsider.

Small speak capabilities are easy methods for building institutions with others. It is tied in with keeping, beginning, and finishing a discourse with colleagues or outsiders.

Small talk is a process for beginning a discussion. Making small talk is a method for accomplishing and interfacing with individuals and expects to provide you contacts with partners, business companions, companions, and others that hold going for a extra drawn-out time frame period.

You might refine the matters, which you wish to mention in the small speak and soon you may discern out that it's miles a powerful and precious method for developing and expanding your agency.

How might you start a verbal exchange with new people you meet at some systems administration occasion or social circumstance? How might you pick out what matters to discuss? Or however, do you preserve on till a number of them stroll directly established upon you? For a few individuals, starting small talk and thinking about icebreakers is a huge problem.

Everything revolves around those off-kilter hushes that make you feel uncomfortable. Thus, while you open your mouth and visually engage, the main factor that rings a bell seems to be inept. Notwithstanding, while you at long ultimate general it thoroughly might be some distance extra detestable. This is where the craft of small communicate comes in.

With the presence of net-based enjoyment, the personal existence of many held individuals has been stepped forward. In any case, in the occasion which you are in a public-confronting role, or you are mastering English as a next language, it's far important to speak with outsiders.

Thus, to assist you with defeating this inclination, we've made a rundown of the excellent small speak factors and inquiries to begin an splendid dialogue resultseasily remoted by means of classifications and going with fashions.

Chapter 2: Why Making Small Talk Is Nothing To Shaggy Dog Story Approximately

There's not anything "little" approximately small communicate.

Having the option to hold a discussion approximately something simple like the weather situations may want to seem as although it's now not great, yet it's crucial information to have within the occasion that you're learning a language. Contemplate how frequently you make small speak on your neighborhood language for the duration of the day.

Making small speak permit you to:

Stay away from peculiar quiets

Effectively get to recognise another individual

Appear to be more amiable

Turn out to be nearer with colleagues and associates

Sound greater like a local speaker

You could make small speak essentially any time you and one (or a pair) others are assembled in a single region, are not occupied and aren't now looking at some thing. You could make casual chitchat at a celebration, earlier than a work meeting, or at the same time as trusting that your meals will microwave inside the place of business.

You can ask a person, or statement on the climate conditions as you are sitting frame, how his morning become whilst you're collectively expecting the boss.

One more high-quality benefit of getting to know English small communicate is that it assists you with beating clumsiness or sensations of humiliation while you are identifying a way to speak in English. Beginning a discussion with an intruder is an extraordinary method for constructing truth, working towards English, and collaborating in small talk. You can speak about the weather, shipping timetable or something else rings a bell!

Non-verbal verbal exchange Is Likewise a Language

Did you assume you have been simply identifying the way to communicate in English here? Your body expresses nearly as a lot as your mouth while you communicate in English — consequently do the collections of others.

For example, assuming you're sitting tight in line to pay for something at the shop, and the character before you is gotten some distance from you, tapping their foot eagerly and searching at their watch continuously, they likely don't have any preference to speak with you. If however, the person before you pivot grabs your interest and grins, you could take a stab at starting a small dialogue.

You could make your self greater congenial through doing little matters that will have a major impact. Assuming you are trying to make small speak, or want to reveal that you're eager on a dialogue, don't fold your palms or your legs. All things being equal, visually join and grin!

Small talk for Each Event

A few topics are all-inclusive, which means you can utilize them wherever and with all people. Others are greater qualified for express occasions. For instance, enterprise-associated topics may be better applied with colleagues at the place of business, and aspect interest-related points can be higher with partners.

Small communicate factors are little — this is, they may be no longer essential or good sized. Keep it certain, and keep away from "weighty" topics, such as anything pessimistic or dubious (a point many individuals differ on).

Try no longer to be excessively irregular, and surprise the opposite man or woman with an unusual new concern. Allow the discussion to take place commonly in preference to attempting to pose inquiries like a rundown. The first-rate small communicate is the situational kind, some thing you see about your cutting-edge condition and work into a discussion.

For instance, you could see the character you are at the carry with that the climate situations are terrible or inquire as to whether he's looking forward to the quit of the week (at the off threat that it's a Friday), yet you likely shouldn't ask him what his side interests are — that is simply weird!

The small conversation is a great problem to pay attention on whether or not you are progressing or truly beginning to research English for fledglings. Peruse directly to discern out the way to casual chitchat like a specialist!

Chapter 3: Small Assist

We can utilize small talk to start discussions with new colleagues or people we know. It is a 'sensitive' approach to getting into a extra extreme dialogue. It regularly would not exactly make any distinction what's being stated. It is a harmless method to laying out an affiliation.

Small speak helps fabricate the established order for genuine discussions and extra profound connections later on. It is an open door. In the event that we ask someone how they are we will dig somewhat greater assuming we're surely intrigued.

A small communicate takes on specific importance when we meet any other accomplice. Establishing a respectable connection is our possibility. Individuals decide us in minutes. Research indicates that it's miles critical to bestow consider and regard in our maximum memorable collaboration to set up a respectable connection.

Our small communicate at our maximum memorable amassing is our opportunity to expose what our identification is.

While the casual discussion is a passage to a dialogue, it's far likewise a period of evaluation. We pick out if the discussion deserves continuing.

Does the opposite man or woman cause us to feel sufficiently outstanding to carry on the dialogue? Is it safe to mention that they may be eager on us?

Individuals who discuss themselves are folks that will usually be egotistical and we might finish we'd as an alternative not continue with the discussion with those individuals. How lots time someone lets in to elapse earlier than they inspect us is a place of energy for their person.

With small communicate, we find the outside layer of our person. We use it to guard our internal ourselves. We permit others to look most effective a tad of us. Truly giving up implies we need to be helpless so we seldom try this whilst we meet any person. We make use of uncontroversial points and mild alternate related to casual banter to preserve quite a few ourselves stowed away.

Here and there casual communication is made just to fill peacefully whilst individuals think of themselves collectively. Quietness can be awkward.

Consummating small communicate

In this point in time, small speak is hard to stay away from. The potential to lead possible small speak is an interactive potential. Certain individuals make easy first institutions with others. Some assume that it's far extra difficult.

Powerful casual discussion will have an impact on us engaging in a part of the things we need to do for the duration of everyday lifestyles.

It could have the impact of locating a new line of labor; marvelous a supervisor in the work surroundings; beginning fellowships and special connections.

You simply get a single possibility to set up the first connection so what you decide to say can be essential. It can require seconds for someone to skip judgment on you and finish whether you advantage conversing with.

By locating multiple trustworthy techniques and expressions, you could determine out how to be wonderful at casual discussion and establish a fantastic first connection.

How to convey with a person

1. Mean to cause the alternative man or woman to feel calm

One aspect to remember whether you do not know in which to begin is to plan to cause the man or woman you're conversing with to sense calm and be in reality keen on them. Praise or popularity them if possible. Plan to fill their coronary heart with pleasure quite greater wonderfully. Grin

2. Listen carefully

Everyone should be paid attention to. So we actually need to listen cautiously to have the choice to present fantastic reactions.

Tune in and pay heed to what people say, and put forth a valiant effort to recollect their call.

Undivided interest implies focusing on what the opposite man or woman is speaking about, in preference to arranging what you'll say straightaway. Posing savvy inquiries is an amazing method for displaying which you're clearly focusing. Individuals want to realize that you care earlier than they may pass on with their discussion.

It's engaging to block out on occasion, but, you'll shape a lot extra grounded institutions in the event which you attention. The different man or woman will see the manner related with you appear.

In any case, there may be an equilibrium. While successfully listening do not deliver the sensation which you carry not anything to the desk within the discussion.

3. Stick to secure points

At the factor whilst we meet new people, it frequently would not make any distinction what's being stated. The problem would not exactly make any distinction. The course of informal dialogue is extensive.

There are sure covered topics that individuals regularly make casual communication approximately. The climate conditions are presumably the principle element that individuals who don't have a clue about one another will take a look at. Another subject this is by way of and massive secure is recent trends the period of it doesn't encompass governmental issues. Sports information is an extremely normal point.

You can honestly relax inside the event that you want to return to the vintage banality subjects as icebreakers — weather, sports activities, visitors, and so forth. You can make use of these as jumping off focuses and hold on from that point to extra charming subjects.

In the occasion that you have something new provide it. Perhaps something has befell to you during the week. You have some other canine. Your baby has stated her maximum memorable phrase. Simply make certain you're veritable.

On the off danger that you can't believe a comment test out you. Track down something to zero in to your environmental elements, just like the piece of expertise at the wall or a fascinating plant. There are in many instances something a good way to begin small communicate and set off subsequent inquiries.

four. Allow the other person to speak first

self assurance and luxury are made when human beings sense apprehended. They need to have the option to speak their thoughts for this to occur.

We must permit the alternative person to speak first. Allow them to start to lead the percent in the dialogue and pose questions to make everything less difficult.

There are times however when you may virtually be brief to begin a discussion with any person and in a while you may need to start it.

5. Pose huge inquiries

You might begin by using essentially asking 'How are you?' yet you could then follow this up with some thing greater large that could start a authentic discussion.

Research shows that people like being asked follow-up inquiries. They view the examiner as being receptive to what they're speakme about.

Start with primary inquiries. These will probably evoke a unmarried-word respond. Then, at that factor, observe with questions that would pass either way that may begin longer and extra extravagant conversations.

In Conversationally Speaking: Tried Better methods to Build Your Own and Social Viability, The following are two or 3 fashions:

"Where are you from?" trailed with the aid of "What is your suburb/metropolis like? How could it be unique on the subject of right here?"

"What do you do?" trailed by using "How could you land up doing that type of work? What do you respect about your paintings?"

Be that as it can, be careful. Assuming you pounce upon the opposite person with questions, they could sense they're being cross-examined.

6. Show authentic interest

Each time you address an person you don't know well, you have a chance to create and increase. Have a certifiable hobby in attending to realize the character you're speaking with and advantage your fine from them.

In the occasion which you display real hobby, you may welcome in addition communication and set up an uplifting vibe for future communications.

7. Be lively.

Regardless of anything or the quantity you assert, your way of speaking, appearance, and eye-to-eye connection will talk a superb deal extra.

It's what you say, yet the manner in which you say it, to be able to help other human beings accomplice with you. Make positive to grin and communicate certifiable energy in the dialogue.

Excitement is infectious. Move towards small communicate emphatically. It might appear to be shallow yet it's far the motive for intending with the dialogue. Assuming you technique informal banter with the conviction that it'll be stupid and silly, it likely may be. Be effective and circulate closer to the circumstance with energy.

eight. Uncover something marginally personal about your self.

You would possibly should provide something of your self in a discussion for the other character to reply and feel sufficiently excellent to attention on themselves. Try not to behave over the top with this or it might make the dialogue off-kilter. You would possibly uncover something about a mindless misstep you as soon as made. Or then again something you are adversely suffering from. It must be pertinent to the dialogue, but, shows a little about what your identity is.

nine. Try now not to over-proportion

However an awful lot we stated you really want to provide some information about yourself, this doesn't suggest you must overshare through the identical token. You might alternatively now not uncover each one in all your mysteries proper on that first connection with them.

Offering some records about yourself is fundamental, but providing a variety of records or a few unacceptable form of facts can kill a discussion faster than nearly whatever else. Keep realities about your self straightforward, and adventure into no hotly debated problems when you're certainly making casual chitchat.

They do not ought to know every one of your exes or family display without skipping a beat. Regardless of your goal with this character, whether or not you're fabricating a fellowship or truly making a dialogue, remain quiet about the considerable records in a few degree for the existing.

10. Know while quietness is becoming

While small speak is the standard for most portions of our lives, there are situations wherein small speak honestly isn't always right - lift rides or passenger trains being extraordinary representations. Regardless of whether or not identifying the way to make small speak is a enormous fundamental capacity, you do not need to utilize it on each odder you run over.

There are simplest situations wherein you don't have to compel a dialogue, and that isn't a problem! It's fundamental to hold an eye fixed out for those expressive gestures, as you will as an alternative not make human beings around you self-conscious.

11. Praise them

Praises do a little first rate matters in making small talk, that's unequivocally why you ought to utilize this on your potential benefit. Let them understand how outstanding they appearance that day or however assuming you absolutely know the critical things approximately them, you could commend their enthusiasm or individual mid-dialogue.

They'll see the value in this method from you and it will likewise marvel them. All the greater considerably, they may be an awesome conversation starter when you're careworn about what to say.

12. Remain off your telephone

Being available within the communique is large. Nowadays that is getting an increasing number of hard to do, so it's far appreciably more esteemed. Remain off your smartphone so you can cognizance at the discussion.

Small speak can also from time to time be ugly however view it as a hazard to greater deeply observe others. No you can actually sincerely inform whom you'll meet or what they will want to proportion.

Grinning and expressing hi to outsiders are strong correspondences and whilst finished reliably will make you a more amiable and congenial man or woman, and increment your bliss.

Chapter 4: For What Purpose Is Small Talk So Significant?

Simply strive and assessment. How may want to you are making a non-herbal dating, a recognizable one? The response to this will be 'small talk.' Utilizing small speak productively close by could make your everyday daily lifestyles fulfillment located and less complicated. You never knew whom you'll meet straightaway.

Whenever you meet a colleague, then these discussions assist you with constructing an splendid creation to your correspondence. It likewise gives you enough room to introduce your thoughts in a fulfilling manner. Other than those, the opposite tremendous motives that help the significance of small communicate are:

1. It makes you extra smart:

According to professionals, such discussions support the critical thinking skills of an person. Hardly any friendly cooperation can incite people to think the exchange way and focus on an trouble with an change point of view and with an exchange association.

2. It is unconstrained:

The best issue about those discussions is that nobody can inform where they will reach, and the opposite extraordinary thing is that it implies no gamble of inclusion. Once in some time, these discussions emerge as being nice to such an extent that they bring about approximately a charming experience or in any occasion, mark the business settlement.

three. It wakes up:

Without a doubt, these discussions light up everything approximately the present. Accordingly, you grow to be greater mindful and consciousness on all that is circumventing you. You may be restricted completely to the cell cellphone, yet this correspondence can help you with acquiring records from other clever personalities within the maximum sincere way.

four. It can assist you with turning into an admirer:

To impact people then it's miles fundamental that you are enjoyed by every certainly one of them. People like those who are safely positive and are liberal to attract in them. You ought to take into account that small talk isn't always just an approach to engaging and trading statistics. It is also a delicate token of regard that most humans recognize.

five. It facilitates you have an progressed outlook on what you're:

Perhaps you aren't an first-rate character, however alternatively definitely every man or woman has a few thrilling qualities that make them no longer pretty the same as others. You can be even not aware of the thrilling competencies that make you now not pretty similar to others, yet these are interior your self and may help you with introducing them to other people.

6. Unavoidably, anybody desires it:

Little discussions are extensive in mild of the reality that nearly everyone needs it. Whether you're arranging any other career in advance or you want to make investments a bit power along with your colleagues, you're marking a essential settlement, or you're in reality engaging your companions, this requires your capacity to participate in small speak.

According to the professionals, your pitch is fundamental in your enterprise to thrive. Indeed, even truthful, innocent visits with the clients are significant. Organizations are continuously chasing after property who can believe the field and little dialogue guidelines help you with questioning the alternate manner.

Chapter 5: Small Subjects

Small speak subjects are excellent ice breakers among folks that do not have a clue approximately one another nicely. Assuming you stay with a social anxiety disease (SAD), making small speak can anxiety incite. It can likewise be difficult assuming you may typically be greater independent.

Figuring out the way to make small communicate can help with building the knowledge you really need to start discussions, make institutions, and foster your social skills. Regardless of whether or not you are awkward, retaining far from small communicate altogether just demolishes uneasiness over the lengthy haul.

Instead of being afraid of small communicate, attempt defeating your apprehension about it. One powerful approach for lightening uneasiness is to apprehend what things to discuss and what to live away from.

Having superb small speak factors at your disposal might not truely assist you with setting out first rate discussions, it will likewise unfastened some from the anxiety of walking into an difficult to understand climate.

1. The location or the setting

Examine your environmental elements. Might or not it's said that you are in a exceptional lodging, domestic, or collecting vicinity? Is the metropolis vital? Did you as of overdue go to somewhere cool nearby?

2. Diversion

Discuss what you have appreciated of late and what's to your rundown. That could incorporate the Netflix show each of you're marathon watching, the closing movie every considered one of you saw, the books you're perusing, the virtual recordings you're streaming, any performs you have joined in, and many others.

3. Craftsmanship

Assuming the man or woman you're addressing appreciates craftsmanship, ask them which historic centers they have long past to and might need to visit, their primary indicates, which specialists they respect, inside the occasion that they've any proposals for exhibitions, which type and car of craftsmanship they like, how their gain created, and so on.

You can likewise have a look at changes inside the craftsmanship global. Are there any latest fads growing they're keen on like "submit-internet workmanship"? What do they sincerely suppose?

four. Food

Food is one of the most splendid small communicate points seeing that almost everyone loves to consume. Ask which cafés that they had suggest and the dishes you ought to arrange. In the occasion that they do not devour out often, ask which dishes they like to make at home. Portray a forthcoming scenario and pay attention their factor of view on what you have to cook or convey. For instance, "I'm accountable for sweet for a housewarming party. There are 10 individuals coming - - two veggie lovers, one person with a nut sensitivity, and some other who does not devour gluten. What may you advise?"

5. Side pastimes

Dig into the other character's pursuits. They'll be excited to talk about what they love, and you'll be capable of interface with them on a greater profound level.

Ask what they do in their to be had strength, which physical games they partake in past paintings and how they have become worried, what their young life entertainment activities were versus now, whether they are taking any instructions, and what they may want to try sushi-manufacturing, novel-composing, salsa moving, and so on.

6. Work

Discussing your day occupations can be precarious. You do not keep that the dialogue should degenerate into an arduous exam of what you do - which it rapidly will besides in case you steer toward a sincerely interesting location.

Then again, paintings is a respectable small communicate subject when you consider that by means of a long way maximum people have a comment.

Rather than posing nonexclusive inquiries like, "Where accomplish your work?" "How lengthy have you ever labored there?" and "Do you want it?", make use of intriguing, startling ones,

7. Sports

Certain people ought to discuss sports activities day in and time out. Others could decide upon to discuss the whole thing except. There are a couple of basic tips for examining sports activities.

To start with, within the event which you're in a meeting of or more individuals, ensure absolutely everyone is an avid supporter. You could alternatively now not keep away from any person from engaging.

Second, whilst an interesting dialogue is a laugh, a warmed one may not help your systems management goals at all. Assuming you or the opposite person beginnings getting provoked up, change the point.

eight. The climate

Weather conditions are a definitive small speak factor. It's typically now not the most glimmering ice breaker, but with a little inventiveness you may begin some drawings in conversations.

Get some statistics approximately the opposite individual's arrangements given the climate for example, in the occasion that it's blustery would they are saying they may remain at home and watch motion images? In the event that it is brilliant, might they are saying they may have a bar-b-que, accomplish something outdoorsy, pass on a climb, have supper on their porch, and so forth?

You can likewise talk approximately their primary sort of surroundings and why they prefer it. This frequently transforms into a conversation about their person, which may be tomfoolery and interest.

Make them discuss the environment in their old neighborhood. Is it no longer pretty the same as wherein they reside now? The equivalent? Which kind do they appreciate extra? In the occasion that they could determine to are living anywhere based exclusively at the atmospheric situations, in which may it's?

Occasional customs and customs are handy ice breakers additionally. Do they do anything precise this season? Are there any spots they visit, journeys they take, individuals they see, or exceptional sporting activities they do?

nine. Travel

Not every body you talk with might be a world voyager, yet inquiring as to whether they have voyaged wherever exciting recently can open up a universe of capacity results. From weekend journeys an hour away to huge summer season tours, or a listing of have to-dos ventures - - this query can get even the maximum stored opportunities spouting about valuable reminiscences or invigorating approaching undertakings.

Ensure you have got some next inquiries approximately what they intend to do on their time out. What food varieties they are generally eager to strive? Furthermore, what items do they're proceeding to deliver again?

10. Their neighborhood pinnacle choices

HubSpot Overseer of Deals Dan Tire has a stunt each rep can make use of. Before a call with a possibility, he researches their city. Frequently, people, he is talking about life in towns Dan's not often visited, however with a two-minute pursuit, he's acquainted with their smoking new café, what the climate conditions are like presently, and which traveler spots neighborhood humans love.

He utilizes this information to wow his possibilities with questions like, "Have you return to Insert up and coming nearby play here yet?" or "Would you say you're final cool around there? I pay attention it'll be inside the '90s this week." This additional step reassures the possibility, shows them Dan thinks often about what they care about, and constructs prompt compatibility.

Chapter 6: Conversation Starter

Whether you are trying to subside into another job or meet another professional contact, the capability to start a dialogue is a tremendous knowledge for systems administration and constructing connections. In any case, it tends to be a take a look at to find the proper phrases each time you first meet someone. No count number what or the individual of the character you need to converse with, there are a few effective techniques for starting a dialogue.

we're going to deliver some fashions you can make use of even as starting discussions.

Step-by using-step instructions to start a dialogue

In the operating surroundings, you may choose exceptional topics to start a discussion for but lengthy they're proper for the weather. Discussions with buddies or professional contacts may be unique in relation to people with new companions or colleagues. Your underlying endeavors ought to begin a dialogue that might repay by assisting you to construct giant associations with collaborators and companions. Here are some ice breakers for the operating environment:

1. Request records

An effective technique for beginning a discussion is to request statistics from the character you need to converse with. This is a a hit, normal approach for building compatibility with any person swiftly. Regardless of whether you really realize the reaction, it's far as but an effective method for moving toward someone within the occasion which you can not believe every other situation.

For instance, at the off risk that you're going to an occasion and see a associate you have not conversed with yet, you may get a few statistics about the collection.

Model: "who became in fee of decoration?"

With this, you may take the dialogue notably similarly via referencing some thing you like approximately the audio system, and so on.

2. Give a pat on the lower back

Praising any individual can light up their day and raise their truth. You can pick some thing approximately the character you want and note why you like it.

Model: "I really like your hair. The reduce fits you."

There are some subsequent inquiries you could pose to transport the dialogue alongside, as an example, in which they visit get their coiffure or how they picked the fashion.

three. Remark on something adorable

You can generally track down something superb to mention concerning an occasion or condition. The occasion might have been the remaining workplace party time or a sporting event that changed into on the earlier night.

Assuming the person gives your views, you're headed to a connecting discussion.

Model: "Did you watch the football match-up the previous nighttime? I suppose our institution, at ultimate, hit their candy spot."

From that factor, the discussion can go in addition into the sport or an extraneous concern, for example, an alternate games institution.

4. Present yourself

While this will now not be affordable for each situation, presenting yourself is a clear approach for displaying your gain in gathering any individual. In the event which you simply began a new position and feature no longer met any individual in any other division yet, you could move in the direction of them and gift your self

Model: "Greetings, I'm Lisa. I'm new to the institution and had to present myself."

You can then ask comply with-up inquiries about their situation or how lengthy they have been with the business enterprise.

five. Offer assistance

In the event that you land up in a situation to assist someone you with desiring to converse with, speedy soar all around the possibility and help them. Offering help can make you affable and gather the agree with of the other character, mainly when you show veritable concern.

Model: "Do you actually need to take a seat?"

From that factor, you may lead right into a dialogue related with the undertaking, as an example, what's inside the items within the folios.

6. Request assist

Mentioning help is every other feasible icebreaker. It works since it encourages the opposite man or woman, specifically at the off threat that it's some thing they can deliver without any problem. In the occasion that anyone facilitates you out, they is probably sure to consider you in a great mild and trust you. Requesting assistance with canning assist you with starting a cordial dialogue however ensure your solicitation is useful for the other birthday party.

Model: "are you able to assist me find the gathering room?"

7. Notice a common encounter

If you have any preference to converse with any individual whom you understand imparts some thing in like manner to you, you could constantly find a theme as an idea. Your commonplace encounters make getting along extra honest and that enables the development of the discussion and the structure of the relationship.

Model: "When did you final see our buddy mickey?" or "How would you want to paintings in Sarah's office?"

eight. Ask for an assessment

Requesting others' viewpoints suggests you esteem and are keen on what they want to say. On the off chance that they recognise approximately the point, many individuals will joyfully solution your inquiries and kick a dialogue off. While inquiring for an assessment, select subjects pertinent to the occasion.

Model: "Are the ones (name emblem) footwear? Is it genuine that they're agreeable?"

nine. Acclaim the individual

At the point whilst you meet a frontrunner or important person in your association curiously, an powerful method for starting a discussion is to laud their paintings.

Model: "I heard the verbal exchange which you gave on the party the remaining week. You made some nice perfect notes."

Follow up the commendation with questions pertinent to the commendation, as an instance, how they became out to be a decent open speaker.

10. Show certifiable hobby

Check whether you may discover a factor you recognise the individual is obsessed on. Interests can get your collaborators talking and you can gain a few new useful understanding. Make positive to maintain the dialogue agreeable and effective.

Model: "I see you're sporting designers. How is it there?"

eleven. Get some information about them

Individuals commonly like discussing themselves. Take a stab at finding a point with a view to permit the individual to speak about their dispositions, family, or encounters.

Model: "How old are your youngsters?" or "I heard which you as of overdue got some margin to go to Hawaii, how became it?"

12. Mention an objective fact

The climate you are in can provide numerous ice breakers. Remarking at the shape, temperature or craftsmanship may be in each way exquisite ways of getting an character speaking to you.

Model: "They labored tough finding the vicinity"

13. Remark at the climate

When in doubt, you could constantly observation on the climate. It is one of the least stressful approaches of having somebody talking and might segue into specific factors.

Model: "It's a pleasing day, isn't always it?" or "Might you at any factor accept all the snow we are getting?"

While assembly new individuals, do you have got any idea a way to make small talk? Do you sense this is the obstacle retaining you lower back from making companions and constructing a public interest? Making small talk is as a remember of fact great know-how to have; it gives you admittance to basically anybody that you run over in a set surroundings.

Vital communique factor

Vital guidelines on the most proficient approach to make small speak and have terrific discussions.

It's way extra truthful than you clearly suspect

What makes small speak simple information to acquire is the way that you can rehearse basically any region. You can rehearse with barkeeps, servers, taxi drivers, buddies, and so on. You can continuously be prepared to speak rather longer with an irregular outsider and take virtually little effort to further develop your small talk muscle.

As a guideline, try to maintain discussions for 5% longer than predicted.

Luckily, you could get higher at it, and it remains with you for quite some time. You naturally start to adjust what you speak and how you do it as in step with the social occasions you're in.

Figure out how To take the path of least resistance

Making small talk is tied in with being abnormal and accepting the way things are. This implies that it's anything however an organized technique for conveying.

The simplest technique for beginning studying small communicate is to apprehend that each one subjects of debate are related. Each subject is connected with each and each other situation, straightforwardly or with the aid of implication. There is consistently a connection among the entirety below the sun else.

For instance, on the off threat that anyone discusses what they noticed on tv nowadays, you could proportion what you taken into consideration as of late on television to be properly. Assuming that they're discussing the information, you could discuss your #1 kind of information, irrespective of whether it is not straightforwardly linked with what they lately referenced.

As a guiding principle, discussing the idea technique helps you to do not forget. Try now not to blue pencil yourself to an excessive...

The adversary of small speak is self-restrict

Since it has come to be so undeniably apparent that each one points are connected, you could begin rehearsing with individuals any place you go.

A sizable block that might not allow you to do that may be a typical inclination to try no longer to explicit your actual thoughts overtly. It's apparent, assuming you simply make statements that are fascinating, fun, unique, interesting, or noteworthy... you will run out of them very quickly.

Rather than blue-penciling your self and completing with not anything to mention, provide your self greater possibility to discover one of a kind avenues concerning topics you are now not used to tending to. You don't need to be Miss or Mister astonishing; you have to clearly get right into a garrulous nation of thoughts.

Presently, wouldn't it be recommended for you to talk about anything that pops as much as you? All matters considered, at the off chance which you enjoy issue making small talk, I wager you are extraordinarily some distance faraway from the other restriction. I wager there are plenty of factors round you, and thoughts you have got inner that you're now not permitting your self to talk about.

I endorse which you damage liberated from that pointless strength of mind and sincerely speak.

Access the enchanted in the back of small speak

An terrific mentality I'll depart you with here is the one where you recognise the really worth of small communicate and why you ought to research it. The motive for shifting discussions along is to bring together compatibility, track down matters in like manner, and cause individuals to experience top.

While it appears to be a few inconsequential gab, small speak has real sorcery behind it. The really worth is in making people OK with you; it makes them confide in extra sizeable discussions. Assuming that there's no small talk and no solace, they live away.

To accomplish that faster, look for inconspicuous shared traits, and spotlight the matters which you settle on with the person. This propensity for figuring out something worth agreeing on with any individual you meet offers you the basis on which you could bring together extraordinary companionships.

Keep in mind, that the basis of companionship is shared traits. Ensure you look for them.

Chapter 7: Introvert Redemption

Introverts will extra regularly than now not fear small talk. They stress that it is going to be exhausting, and strange, or that they may run out of feedback.

Be that as it is able to, in this day and age, small talk is tough to stay far from. Mixed drink events, organizing activities, and, tremendously, the road for coffee at paintings might require a quick exchange of merriments.

Many Introverts could be taken aback to discover that small talk doesn't need to be agonizing. By studying multiple sincere strategies, you can clean your conversational abilties and establish a fantastic connection.

The following are tips to becoming the exceptional at small communicate.

1. Diminish anxiety.

Introverts would possibly pass toward small talk with tension, going from mild worry to incapacitating worry. One loner allow me understand that he conceals within the washroom or fiddles with his cellphone to avoid inactive gab. To control your anxiety, stay sane and high quality. Let your self recognise any of the accompanying

"The stress this is coming from my thoughts and me, and not the situation am in. I can try this."

"What's the more terrible that may occur? In the event that they could do with out me, so what?"

"That what transpires earlier than does no longer suggest it'll take region again."

"Names do not symbolize me. I'm an exciting, commendable person with a ton to make a contribution.

2. Be planned.

Considerations will quite frequently be inevitable. Assuming you technique small speak with the conviction that it is going to be stupid and futile, it probable will. Rather than harping on regrettable contemplations, advocate yourself that small communicate isn't always shallow. Small speak fills a full-size need - it enables assemble the establishment for bona fide discussions and extra profound connections no longer too a long way off. Consider small speak the light hors d'oeuvre earlier than the fundamental route, and flow towards it with restored cause.

three. Channel your hobby.

Introverts will normally be involved people. They love digging profound, diving into subjects that interest them, and knowing what's maximum essential to people. Channel your regular hobby into small communicate. At the point whilst you question "how's it going?" or "did you have an awesome week?", move toward the discussion with licensed hobby. Cautiously take note of the subsequent person, and give an insightful response. In the event which you show proper hobby, you will welcome in addition communication and establish an uplifting vibe for destiny cooperation.

four. Seek rationalization on some pressing issues.

Introverts will more regularly than not sense awkward on the middle of interest. They are regularly hesitant to show a lot about themselves, especially to new people. So how may you start discussions and preserve them streaming? The reaction is easy - are seeking rationalization on a few pressing troubles. By allowing the alternative person to emerge as the overwhelming awareness at the beginning, you can assemble your solace level and strive things out prior to sharing your own contemplations. Assuming that you are feeling awkward or exhausted mid-dialogue, pose more inquiries and unobtrusively disregard the attention from yourself. Be that as it may, do not be enticed to permit the opposite individual to speak the whole thing! See tip

5. Add scrumptious sweets.

On the off danger that you tirelessly pepper the opposite man or woman with questions, it's going to feel like a pass-examination. Sooner or later, you have to proportion a bit approximately yourself. Try not to give a single word, or close reaction; these cut the dialogue off. All matters being identical, enhance your reactions with scrumptious sweets of facts. By giving multi-layered reactions, you could supply "snares" for the alternative individual to continue with the dialogue. For instance:

Question: "How are you?" Short reaction: "good enough." Better response: "grand, plenty valued. I'm making ready for my tour to Britain. It may be my most memorable time in Europe, and I expect attempting valid English tea."

Question: "Where are you from?" Short response: "Seattle." Better reaction: "I'm from Seattle. It would not rain constantly, and I partook inside the outstanding fish and coffee. There are Starbucks everywhere."

Question: "How become the week?" Short response: "I to search for a residence." Better reaction: "I went residence-looking, we're considering the metropolis versus suburbia. We can get extra houses in suburbia, yet the compromise is the drive."

6. Develop the discussion.

Basic inquiries will generally encourage a unmarried-word reply. Inquiries with out a right or incorrect answer, however, can begin longer and greater extravagant conversations. Begin with truthful inquiries. All things taken into consideration, you'll rather now not frighten the opposite man or woman off. In Conversationally Speaking: Tried Better approaches to Build Your Own and Social Adequacy, Alan Earn proposes following up basic inquiries with unconditional ones. Questions that might move either manner can poke the dialogue into the extra profound, greater actual area - in which considerate humans will typically flourish.

7. Perceive activates.

Introverts are regularly misjudged. Others might decipher the contemplative character's held nature as snobbish, or they could song down an Introvert's profound enthusiasm for a selected difficulty to be excessively brilliant or serious. As an Introvert, you can look for signals and figure out how to properly answer. For instance, assuming that the opposite man or woman seems to be shocked by your held nature, ensure to grin and speak veritable energy in the dialogue. Or then again on the off danger that the other person begins to get restless at the same time as you are talking for a long term concerning a matter, it's probable an possibility to trade to one more point or wrap up the dialogue.

8. Be thoughtful to your self.

Introverts are typically contemplative spirits who can think for extensive stretches of time. Nonetheless, this present can turn into a revile when thoughtful human beings harp on their personal apparent flaws and disappointments. On the off threat that a particular challenge went poorly, Introverts would possibly replay the episode to them and scold themselves for not doing matters another way. In the occasion that you messed up a discussion or wish you hadn't said both, require multiple moments to contemplate and deal with your "focal point" instance for some time later. Then essentially allow it pass. No one's ideal. To gain anything wonderful, you have to bomb usually and periodically appearance mindless previous to making development.

Chapter 8: Bad Aspect

The difficulty, obviously, is that small communicate goes before the big speak within the traditional direction of human undertakings. The full-size majority want to emerge as familiar with every other before they bounce into the profound end of significant discussion or progressing kinship. And that implies on the off danger which you disdain and avoid small communicate, you're likewise, as an inexpensive depend, casting off yourself from heaps of significant social connection, that is a bummer. Likewise, it suggests that more continuous small talk, even a number of the folks that recognize as loners, makes individuals more comfortable. Additionally, notwithstanding ongoing advances in innovation, small speak stays an simple piece of severa vital life undertakings.

So it might be best to be better at small speak, or in all likelihood to recognize the purpose why a few are so horrendous at it. We should look at the exploration.

Scientists recognize that small talk isn't any little element

For all its omnipresence, the small communicate hasn't come in for a lot of scholastic opinions. It is discourse as pleasant conserving instead of correspondence.

To a characteristic guy, any other man's quietness is sincerely no longer a consoling variable, on the identical time, going for walks towards the norm, some thing disturbing and unsafe. They are anticipated to move beyond the bizarre and horrendous stress that men feel whilst confronting each different peacefully.

For pretty a long time from that point, small talk held its status as the least kind of discourse, a simple area filler to keep away from quiet, minimum deserving of regard or extreme assessment.

During the 1970s, anyhow, sociolinguistics grew to become out to be extra sensitive to the everyday kinds of discourse that, all things considered, include the heft of our verbal correspondence. Furthermore, ladies's activist sociolinguistics especially observed that a cavalier demeanor toward a discourse that lays out and maintains up with connections — as opposed to undertaking-situated or academic discourse — changed into of a bit with guy-centric dismiss for normally lady jobs. Consider the slanderous ramifications of the expression "tattle," which is, all matters taken into consideration, social discussion about friendly factors.

What basically rises up out of women's activist scrutinizes is the manner that western social orders have earnestly mentioned that correspondence is as a count number of truth esteem gradable, on a scale from maximum-to-least real or maximum-to-least good sized. ... Whether "proper talk" has been held to take care of commercial enterprise' selective area is, according to this perspective, less large than the manner that an evaluative public origination of correspondence itself is unequivocally set up. The actual communicate may be a discussion that "finishes stuff," where "stuff" does exclude "social stuff."

In present-day sociolinguistics, there's been quite a few academic research of "social language" and the severa circumstances where small communicate assumes a extensive proscribing part.

small communicate isn't most effective full-size for the ones seeking out friendship or maintaining away from quietness. It's likewise massive in an entire scope of social, business, and professional settings. It winds round and reweaves the social texture, instituting and building up friendly jobs.

Each has its own rhythms and regulations. Furthermore, glaringly, the persona of informal conversation contrasts from one spot to some other, culture to culture. For instance, quietness isn't always seen as compromising or awkward in all societies.

Discourse talks, yet it likewise receives things done

We really want not to get excessively far within the weeds. At a general stage, it is essentially critical to don't forget that every discourse act works on two ranges. On one level, it imparts statistics or thoughts. This is the semantic substance of the discourse,

On another stage, speaking is a social way of behaving. Each discourse act is an indication, implied not solely to impart something yet to comply with via with some thing: reassure, understand, sustain, charge, reject, rule, support, or without a doubt fill off-kilter quietness. We can don't forget this the social functionality of a discourse act. Dissimilar to semantic substance, social functionality cannot be grasped in that body of thoughts, by using studying the words. Social functionality is based altogether upon setting, tone, and non-verbal conversation, relational jobs being played, on true and natural activates. It just seems OK compared with the putting.

All discourse acts work on the 2 ranges, but the proportion of social functionality to semantic substance contrasts along a continuum. In positive situations, discourse acts take on a predominantly open process: a consultant portraying her clinical manner; an observation pilot depicting troop trends; a college speaker portraying an episode of history.

Be that as it may, instances of simply open discourse are greater the exemption than the same old, tracked down particularly expert or scholarly settings. As sociolinguists have come to comprehend, in everyday human communication discourse is a social, social way of behaving. That is the purpose regular examples and ceremonies of discourse honestly deserve take a look at; they uncover the social texture.

Small talk falls on the other finish of the continuum; discourse makes a speciality of friendly functionality. Consider this change: "How's it going?" "Gracious, very awesome."

There's now not zero semantic substance in there — reputedly "very fantastic" bars "kicking the bucket at this cautious 2nd," so that is a few information. Yet, the critical functionality of these discourse acts is social, no longer to mention something but instead to observe via with some thing, i.E., connect, reaffirm shared enrollment in a standard clan, something it very well might be, express top sentiments and subsequent absence of hazard, show concern, and so on. These aren't insignificant matters, now not "little" via any way, truely, however, they may be no longer pretty the same as supplying semantic substance.

Small communicate — particularly in its maximum ideal structure, phatic fellowship — is a placing wherein language has a proper pleasant. The correspondence of mind or records is optional and practically coincidental; the discourse is essentially supposed to fill the want for social conserving. It asks and addresses natural inquiries, stays on subjects of strong comity, and stresses character inclination as opposed to wellsprings of struggle.

In opposition to everyday recommend to "keep it light," concentrates on showing that people want having similarly and more vast conversations. In addition, taking part in meaningful discussions is hooked up with extra outstanding bliss and prosperity. There are two essential clarifications for this — we're importance looking for creatures and we are social creatures. Chatting approximately our encounters and our wellknown environment empowers us to track down significance in our lives. Great discussions likewise paintings withholding and a extra prominent affiliation with the individual with whom we are talking. Basically, attempting to discuss stuff that topics is a sincere method for growing bliss.

Chapter 9: Understanding The Small Talk Mindset

Without a doubt, it can be difficult for lots human beings to make small talk. The pressure of being in a room full of strangers can quick develop into a dire situation for introverts and shy human beings alike. You may additionally find yourself heading off eye touch so as to avoid having to interact in communication.

When it involves small talk, we've discovered to push aside it as trivial and missing in conversational price. Ultimately, how we've found out to peer and exercise a conversation can make it poisonous-- now not the exercise of communique itself. In different words, what you assert and the way you are saying it are various things. The latter can be extra important in this situation. To be proper at talking, you want to put in as a lot attempt into listening as you do speakme. The concept of small talk would possibly seem sparse, till you understand all that a conversation can embody. Practicing small communicate in a way that advantages you and the other man or woman involved is one of the most essential skills everyone can increase.

Using small communicate as a cowl for no longer announcing what we suggest is a common incidence in social conditions. Small talk questions elicit automatic responses from us due to our social conditioning. As long because the communique is effective, it is viable to get a number of value out of it, no matter whether or not it is with a entire stranger or a pal. These are valuable moments that should no longer be taken for granted. Still, maximum human beings aren't inclined to open up to each other approximately their deepest, darkest secrets and techniques or the that means of existence, so small communicate is essential to begin the procedure of building a connection. Remember that every now and then the best matters in lifestyles could have the best effect.

The four Basic Stages of Conversation

When we start a new paintings assignment, attend social gatherings or end up involved in our neighborhood network, we generally meet new humans. Therefore, it's far vital that we learn how to set up proper running relationships from day one. True conversational talent includes now not handiest knowing when to say the proper component but also understanding whilst no longer to.

When it involves getting to know someone, small speak both lubricates the conversation or acts as a barrier.

You ought to realize while to say the perfect aspect, but additionally whilst to hold the incorrect object out of the verbal exchange. This is an important a part of conversational mastery. At this point within the dating, discretion is needed. Your consolation degree with the other person is significantly encouraged by way of this movement.

We engage in communique at one of a kind levels of intimacy depending on how nicely we recognize the other individual. By being attentive to those four stages of focus, we are able to either begin a relationship off on the right foot or doom it from the get-cross.

Let's take a closer take a look at each:

1. Small Talk

The first stage of verbal exchange is known as small speak, that is what this e book is set. It's common to apply small speak as a way to get humans talking about matters they're interested in. It's possible that we are going to talk approximately the climate, our modern-day location, or cutting-edge events.

A character's consolation stage is installed at some point of the small speak degree. Additionally, it provides an possibility for people to 'size up' one another in a nonjudgmental surroundings and decide whether or not they want to invest time and energy in the interaction or courting.

Building consider and rapport can take time, however small talk is an essential a part of the manner. If the small speak is going well (and you've internalized the principles in this e-book) you may then move on to the next stage.

2. Fact Disclosure

At this stage, you could proportion some non-public information about your self, along with in which you grew up or what you like about your enterprise. At this degree, your aim is to get to know the alternative man or woman better, and with the aid of doing so, you're extending the trust you've got already constructed with him or her.

After comfort is set up in this phase, you may continue to the 0.33 stage.

3. Common Ground

During this section, the goal is to try and locate points of settlement with the alternative individual. In this second, it's a good idea to invite the alternative man or woman about their non-public interests or taste in music, sports or food.

It's vital that the preceding steps have long gone easily so that you can depend upon your relationship to act as a buffer now. You do not need to get into a fight over personal options earlier than you've got even had a risk to get to recognise each different.

There are motives why you need to finish levels 1 and 2 before shifting on to this one: First and important, people need to build accept as true with earlier than discussing sensitive topics that might motive offense if misunderstood. Second, sharing one's thoughts and ideas exposes one to scrutiny, so one should have faith within the different man or woman to start with. It is viable to progress to the subsequent stage if this one goes nicely.

4. Personal Feelings

This stage includes the expression and recognition of 1's very own innermost thoughts and feelings.

Before this level, consider and rapport must had been built up between the two humans worried. First-stage conversation will assist you form appropriate running relationships and permit you to proportion deeper ranges of records along with your coworkers or capacity colleagues without risking them being misunderstood. Achieving this stage of communication within the workplace is vital to maximizing your collaborative efforts. Establishing a terrific running relationship through powerful verbal exchange will assist you feel extra relaxed while discussing both minor and foremost problems in business.

Why Small Talk Triggers Anxiety

On the floor, small speak seems like it have to be smooth, however it is now not always that easy and there are a number of reasons why it could be hard. Despite the fact that a few people enjoy speakme approximately themselves, this show of openness does no longer usually occur amongst strangers.

As a baby, we're taught that we should not have interaction in communique with people we don't know. This rule, at the start designed to hold us safe, has remained with most of us into adulthood.

In public, we hold our thoughts to ourselves. We do not regularly appearance to interact with others if on a bus or train. We generally tend to keep away from attractive with strangers at social gatherings, preferring to speak with the few human beings we understand instead of taking a chance on a communique with a person we don't.

When we do engage with strangers, these conversations revolve round weather, lengthy strains, or delayed buses.

Small speak evokes photos of awkwardness and soreness in our minds. There is a fear of being rejected or feeling like you've got nothing in common with a stranger when you try and begin a conversation. People we don't know or count on aren't interested in what we've to mention, could make it tough to strike up a verbal exchange with them.

While most human beings can effortlessly solution questions about their lives, many people select no longer to guide the communication. The fact is, most folks honestly have a hard time being open. It's a crimson flag while two human beings start a communique and each claims to be the one doing the listening. As a result, the interaction can become strained as both parties try and get the opposite to open up.

A productive conversation looks a lot distinctive. Conversations tend to run more without problems whilst both individuals are listening attentively and elaborating on every other's thoughts. This adds intensity to a dialogue and expands on topics, bringing collectively the pastimes and curiosity of both parties. Both talkers and listeners end up concerned in the verbal exchange. This can go greater smoothly if there are two "talkers," or if there's a talker who is a good listener. Small speak is no longer an option when you're engaged on this form of interaction due to the fact real verbal exchange is taking place right here.

It's common for human beings to make assumptions about other human beings's attitudes primarily based on their personal behavior. When all and sundry isn't speaking, it's clean to count on that no one desires to speak, but this is now not usually the case. As a end result, we're unable to form significant relationships with new people.

The University of Chicago's Nicholas Epley and Schroeder concluded that folks who engage with strangers are more satisfied than folks who do not. Commuters on trains and public buses, passengers in taxis, and people in a simulated waiting room were all blanketed in the examine. By creating a "ready room"-like setting, the researchers examined if the favorable influences of social connection extended to folks that have been spoken to.

The researchers concluded that conversations with strangers on public transportation have been more fun for folks who had been advised to interact in communique in place of stay silent.

Why introverts hate small talk

"I hate small speak" is a word many human beings use. If you're one of them, you're probable an introvert. Psychologist Laurie Helgoe claims that introverts despise small communicate because it creates a barrier among them and the people they want to connect with. In other phrases, human beings do not get to understand each other because of superficial, polite communique.

Introverts commonly dislike small communicate for the following reasons:

· They opt for long, in-intensity conversations with a small institution of people. They agree with it's unnecessary and tedious to have interaction in a verbal exchange approximately meaningless subjects.

· Small speak seems phony to them. Why waste time and effort in case you're not interested by making a reference to all of us? It doesn't feel right.

· Small communicate is regularly characterized by using egotistical ramblings. Introverts tend to be more humble and accept as true with that people who experience small speak the most opt for to talk approximately themselves and their accomplishments in preference to specializing in others.

· For an introvert, the worry of being placed instantaneous can be overwhelming if you do not know what to mention. Introverts generally tend to manner mind internally, while extroverts choose to consider matters from afar. When an introvert has to provide you with an "immediately answer" to a question, they may feel less confident.

· Finally, spending time with others drains the power of introverts, and they commonly choose to use that electricity on something extra effective.

In this section, you discovered approximately what compromises a verbal exchange and why many people fear undertaking small communicate. In the next chapter, we are able to speak the most common worry people have when carrying out light communique – being judged.

Chapter 10: Overcoming The Fear Of Judgment

Socialized anxiety disorder is characterized through an extreme dread of being judged in social instances. Regardless of ways steady we feel, we all have those moments while we are fearful of what others might imagine. When we're frightened of how others understand us, it is regular to tighten up or maintain lower back our thoughts when speaking. This tension may gift itself as a desire to please others on the fee of 1's very own convictions. However, when you know you won't be capable of please every person, it is probably difficult to come to a decision. Many folks worry that others will find fault with the issues we see in our own selves. Critical mind come to be part of our focus.

Fortunately, small speak tension may be alleviated by way of the usage of the cognitive restructuring ability to trade your questioning so that it is greater realistic, beneficial, and compassionate.

You can in the end gain self assurance and reduce your worry of small communicate in case you face it head on.

For cognitive restructuring to be powerful, you need to be capable of perceive the thoughts which might be causing you misery and take action to relieve them. Keeping song of whilst and where your mind stand up is another helpful device.

In some settings, you'll be greater susceptible to cognitive distortions. You can better prepare your self if you are aware about these potential situations. When you are aware about your own vulnerability, you are higher capable of seize your self in a terrible idea cycle and make a aware effort to regulate it.

Journaling may be beneficial for sure human beings all through the process. No be counted how harassed or disturbing you are, preserving a magazine may help you perceive a pattern of questioning that is contributing on your distress.

The following steps need to be taken which will efficiently interact in cognitive restructuring. Doing so will permit you to allow go of your personal self-prejudices and start to interact in powerful small speak with strangers.

1. Take a Hard Look At Your Own Preconceptions

Learning to observe your perspectives and assumptions, specially those who seem to come in the way of leading a efficient lifestyles, is a important thing of cognitive restructuring.

The Socratic method of inquiry, which a therapist can train you, will help you discover the biases and incorrect assumptions that run rampant to your thoughts.

Some questions to recall consist of:

·Does this belief stem from emotions or facts?

·What are the worst-case eventualities?

·What would be the quality route of movement if the worst have been to show up?

·Is there some other manner to take a look at this statistics?

·Is there any proof that this bias is true?

·Is there any evidence that this bias isn't actual?

Many of our biases are primarily based in a behavior called catastrophizing, which can be described as a form of cognitive distortion wherein human beings assume the worst ability results beneath stressful conditions. Question this sample of wondering by using creating a list of all potential effects. As a start line, you can do not forget how manageable every situation is.

2. Collecting Information

Gathering evidence is an critical a part of cognitive restructuring. Keep tune of the occasions that cause you to react, which include where you have been and what you had been doing at that point. You can also want to hold tune of the depth of your reactions and the recollections that got here to mind.

Alternatively, you might gather evidence to help or disprove your evaluations and assumptions. Biased and misguided, cognitive distortions can also be profoundly ingrained. In order to dispose of and replace them, proof of their rationality is required.

You may additionally need to collect a list of information that support a perception, after which examine this to a listing of facts that disprove the concept.

As an instance, if you subconsciously claim other humans's moves as your very own, you can emerge as blaming your self for matters that aren't definitely your fault. Look for information that suggests an motion isn't always associated with you in any manner.

Even if we want to feel much less fearful and more comfortable when talking to others, we should also change our mindset. We have a tendency to rely upon behavioral crutches on the way to deal with our anxieties. Short-time period comfort from anxiety may also come from these safety-in search of actions. However, they can reason us to feel extra stressful in the end due to the fact our self-talk can cross awry. Also, they hold us from figuring out that our nagging doubts and self-defeating mind are just that: nagging.

Safety Seeking Behaviors & Their Remedies

Small communicate tension is normally preceded through many distinct varieties of conduct which might be controlled by using cognitive dissonance. Next, we will evaluate the maximum not unusual protection-seeking practices together with guidelines on a way to treatment every behavior.

1. Being Overly Cautious

This is an typical safety-seeking approach in which we're very cautious and scared of taking dangers whilst we talk to humans. Using this technique is primarily based on our notion that humans will disapprove people if we're now not flawless. This notion leads us to apply all varieties of behavioral crutches, which includes all of these listed on this section. Being very careful may keep us from making a mistake every now and then, however it often stops the communique from flowing and makes us experience tons greater aggravating.

Remedy: Be More Carefree & Take Social Risks

This can be frightening before everything, however after you get used to it, freedom is observed. Gradually permit your guard down, chat openly, and push yourself from your comfort area. This makes conversations go with the flow extra smoothly and enables others hook up with you. You'll learn that, regardless of your imperfections, you have got accurate conversational talents and maximum humans revel in conversing with you. If you by chance insult or embarrass someone, say "I'm sorry, I failed to imply to" or "Oops, I say silly things from time to time." Then, preserve speaking even as listening to the other person and what they're saying—all the even as treating yourself-judgment and terrible feelings like history noise. You'll possibly analyze that errors are simply bumps in the road and things cross again to ordinary fast.

Your obsessive thoughts and primary beliefs may be tested even in addition by means of organizing a series of "social blunder experiments" in which you purposefully choose to commit an blunders in communication. You ought to say which you forgot the character's call or use the wrong call on cause throughout the interaction. You can ask the other person some thing they have already instructed you or repeat a statement you've already said. You can lie about what you understand or fake you do not know. You might be clumsy on purpose, exchange your thoughts on reason, or make an deliberately stupid request. You may want to make your self blush, sweat, or feel jittery on reason, or you may just say which you're nervous for the duration of the conversation.

After you're making a mistake, make a light, planned remark to make it seem like not anything came about. Don't be protective or too apologetic, after which keep on with the verbal exchange as though nothing took place. You'll locate evidence that being improper is regular and that most humans don't care and still get along with you. Paradoxical experiments may be frightening before everything, but they tend to be amusing and regularly humorous, and they assist you get away from the pressures of perfectionism over the years.

2. Scripting

This conduct is what we do when we're uncertain what to say subsequent in a conversation (or even earlier than it starts). This is once in a while useful, but most of the time it keeps us from listening carefully, which stops our brains from arising with thoughts on their own in response to what's being stated. Scripting is tough work and reinforces the concept that you need to do things perfectly to be exact sufficient, which makes you less happy and more annoying. Scripting additionally makes conversations awkward and stilted, in preference to flowing clearly.

Remedy: Free Association

Pay attention to what's being said right now, not what you need to say next. Don't write down what you want to say. Instead, say some of the things that come to thoughts as you pay attention to the character, the communique, and the things going on around you. Be confident in your mind. Your mind will cope with the assignment for you if you do not disturb it with any scripting. Listen with interest, after which proportion your thoughts or ask questions after you have had some time to method what you heard. During a lull in the communique, recollect the remaining statement said or the person who stated it, and then continue the conversation from there. If you find that your free association is leading you in a specific course, you should not be hesitant to switch gears and change the topic. This sort of natural wandering keeps social conversations thrilling. Dropping the crutch of scripts might be horrifying before everything, however it's going to get less difficult as you display that you could keep a conversation well enough whilst you pay interest.

three. Interviewing

Do you regularly try to avoid being the middle of attention by means of asking a number of questions and no longer announcing lots about yourself? Questions show which you care and may be useful, however simplest up to a point. A long listing of questions, alternatively, can make each people feel worn-out and turn a communication into an uncomfortable interview. It makes us less glad, makes it more difficult to connect with other human beings, and makes us extra positive that different human beings wouldn't want to speak to us.

Remedy: Lead a Balanced Discussion

Make it a goal to speak approximately yourself as much as the other man or woman. Don't maintain a near eye in this, though. That might just take your mind off being curious and listening to the communique. Instead, be barely aware of how a great deal you and the opposite character is saying and displaying. If you sense such as you don't say as a good deal as the alternative person (or that you typically react to different human beings and say little about yourself) make a change. Speak up extra frequently and allow humans recognise more approximately your self. If you feel like you are speaking lots longer than other man or woman—ask a question or two. People can connect to you a lot higher whilst the communique is extra or less even than whilst you try to change the challenge. Even although this will be difficult in the beginning, it's going to help you display that people like speakme to you in standard.

4. Avoidance

Too often, we do not do things we need to do because we're involved or having negative thoughts. It could be as obvious as no longer going to activities, no longer beginning conversations with human beings, or no longer joining institution discussions. It can also be greater diffused-- like now not speakme a whole lot approximately yourself, not giving your opinion, or cutting short conversations. There are also many nonverbal approaches to attempt to avoid attention, like averting eye touch or talking softly or with out displaying emotion.

Overt avoidance may assist us sense much less aggravating for a short time, but it charges us loads. Avoidance makes our bad mind and middle beliefs stronger, keeps us from figuring out how incorrect they are, and makes us extra tense the next time.

Remedy: Make Progress By Taking Small Steps Forward

If you've previously prevented doing something due of your tension, set tiny however common desires to step out of your consolation region. Be sure to pay attention to the person, communication, or activity as you do these items. By taking small steps forward, you'll find increasingly more proof that your terrible mind and center beliefs are incorrect. This will help you experience much less anxious and more confident through the years.

Set new dreams for non-verbal avoidance patterns which include organising extra eye touch, talking stronger and with more expressiveness, and smiling greater. But make sure you are listening to the communique itself and now not to yourself and how you are appearing.

five. Being Naturally Silent

When you say some thing or solution a query, do you generally tend to mention it quickly? This is a commonplace manner to keep away from being judged by getting humans's attention off of ourselves. But in case you do that lots, it tends to annoy the alternative character, who is handiest trying to speak to you and might need to examine more approximately you.

Remedy: Telling Stories and Speaking More Broadly

Make it a goal to mention greater than just a few phrases almost whenever you communicate to someone in a social setting.

It does not take plenty more work, however it makes it more likely that someone will hook up with what you assert and that the conversation will go with the flow. If someone wonders how you are doing, saying "high-quality" terminates the conversation. Say as an alternative, "Okay. I cannot wait for the weekend due to the fact work is annoying." With only a little more paintings, you may bring up different topics—work, stress control, sleep conduct, films, and books— which could result in more verbal exchange and increase your possibilities of connecting with a person. Also, each sometimes, tell a short story approximately some thing you've got performed or visible. This keeps humans involved and helps them get to recognise you higher.

When you proportion information, you're much more likely to engage others. Yes, speakme lots and telling tales keep humans's attention on you for longer, that's probable to make you sense more stressful in the beginning. Instead of residing to your fears, consciousness on the existing second and you will find out that maximum people revel in talking with you and that your communique talents are enough.

6. Introspection and Self-Analysis

Have you ever experienced an internal "self critic" while talking to a person? Have you observed your self judging the way you thought you appeared and acted? You might deliver immoderate attention on your anxiety signs and symptoms to try and manipulate them and appear calm. People who have social tension frequently compare and go-take a look at themselves. Even though those symptoms are meant to help us get higher, they take our attention away from the verbal exchange and make it a lot more difficult to participate. They additionally make us frightened, ashamed, or unhappy.

Remedy: Mindfulness

Practicing mindfulness, that's the most important and underappreciated social talent, is the first-class remedy for this problem. It's vital to word that Mindfulness isn't always the same as meditation. However, meditation is one way to practice mindfulness. The term "mindfulness" refers back to the act of focusing one's interest at the present day moment as opposed to on something in the past or future. Mindfulness for social anxiety is being attentive to the person, the conversation, and the pastime within the right here and now with a sense of hobby. Distracting mind and feelings then come to be not anything greater than background noise. This is typically called idea defusion. Engaging in this conduct shall we us take part inside the verbal exchange in a greater natural way and experience it extra.

Mindfulness can be practiced in our every day interactions by using engaging in interest training. When we are distracted by mind or emotions, we can lightly bring our interest back to the person, the communication, or the activity in the gift. When you're comfortable, you could already do that on your very own. The extra you exercise, the simpler it turns into to cognizance at the contemporary second as opposed to focusing in your thoughts and emotions even as you feel burdened.

In this chapter, we found out the numerous ways that fear and bad wondering hinders our ability to make small communicate. In the subsequent chapter, you may learn how to make a strong and fantastic first impact when assembly new humans.

Chapter 11: Making First Impressions

There is not anything greater critical than making a very good first influence in each social activities and the paintings location. Since we've got brief, primordial brains, you want to set the opposite person's thoughts comfortable in order to technique you. According to maximum experts, a first impression may be made in seven seconds. Some of the maximum important components of first impressions consist of:

·Appearance

·Manners

·Body language

·Conversation

·Attentiveness

Even though small talk may also seem insignificant before everything, learning the artwork should result in super matters. It's vital to make the maximum of the first few minutes of a brand new courting because they've so much capacity.

Research suggests that we can choose someone's splendor and trustworthiness inside the time it takes to blink our eyes. In the subsequent three seconds, we form a more "complete" opinion approximately a brand new pal primarily based on what we consider their character and potential.

In that quick of a time, it's clear that we have not simply gotten to recognise every other. Instead, we've got made a "snap judgment" about someone based totally on our cognitive biases and filters, simply as they have finished approximately us.

Those critiques can also or won't be right, but they stick round. And if the opinion is poor, it's far very hard to exchange.

In a lot of ways, making snap choices primarily based on first impressions is just like the halo effect, that's when you see precise characteristics in one factor or element after which see those same features in associated things or the entire.

So, it is vital to recognize the way to make a higher first impression and improve your chances of doing so. Most of the time, human beings communicate with out words. This method that how we look, how we sound, and the way we scent have plenty to do with the primary impressions we make on new humans.

What we do with our bodies is a great deal extra important than what we are saying.

Making a Good First Impression

People tend to love others who are like them in appears, persona, mind-set, ideals, and behavior, whether they're aware of it or now not. The first impact a person has people is likely to be laid low with how we look, talk, and act.

People frequently mistakenly trust that others proportion their ideals and beliefs. This is a gain of the doubt that we should not violate by displaying a person we simply met how exclusive we're early on.

The essential attribution bias is certainly one of the largest cognitive biases human beings have. We tend to characteristic the actions of others to their inherent trends or incompetence, however we tend to attribute our personal movements more to our environment and outside circumstances.

First impressions ultimately rely on some of biases.

Here are only some of the precise objects that research has shown have an impact on human beings's first impressions of latest humans they meet. It's vital to keep in thoughts that these are just habits and inclinations, not conclusions that everybody involves.

Take the following observed behaviors and their most in all likelihood first impact into attention:

Straight posture

- > They are equipped and centered.

Physical splendor

-> They are healthful or higher than me.

Appearing smart or wealthy

- > They must be influential or vital.

Strong eye touch

-> They are, maximum possibly, wise.

First impressions are essential, so right here are a few basic guidelines for setting up an excellent one when you meet a person new:

·Dress a bit higher than the event calls for.

·Make eye touch regularly, specially while you're speaking, but don't allow your eyes take over.

·Smile, on account that it can be observed from a first rate distance.

·Focus on the character's great exceptional to position you in a advantageous body of thoughts.

·Adapt your voice, body language, posture, and phrases to in shape the alternative person considering that we prefer human beings similar to us.

·Give people the hazard to prove you wrong based totally on their very own biases.

·Early on, venture what you need to say most approximately your self.

When it involves developing first impressions, there is most effective one hazard to make an excellent one. But that should not make you afraid of them.

Projecting Confidence

Although thoughts and feelings can impact one's moves, this isn't usually the case. If we allow our body take the lead, our thoughts will comply with healthy. Imagine how could you feel bodily if you were assured on your message. Would you increase your shoulders, smile, and keep eye touch for an extended time frame? Would you take into account speakme extra slowly? Deeper?

Imagine a person who's confident in their own skills, and ask yourself what they look or sound like. It doesn't count in case you accept as true with it or not, pretending to be assured is a outstanding way to triumph over shyness or the awkward first five minutes of communication.

If you want to make a lasting impact, bear in mind that it's now not your phrases that stick inside the minds of your target audience, but the manner you're making them experience. All brilliant things start with a small beginning. After some crazy, awkward moments, you can be in your manner somewhere.

Using the FORM Method

As formerly stated, human beings are attracted to people who share their pastimes. However, it may nonetheless be tough to strike up a conversation with a stranger about something in common. So how do you even begin? What happens in case you don't percentage any interests? Conversation could also be hampered by the reality that you see the identical character on a regular basis. With everyday friends, consisting of co-people, classmates, and spouses with whom you share a domestic and family, you could discover it tough to give you new topics of conversation to percentage.

The FORM technique is a conversational approach that enables you conquer awkward moments of silence with friends, coworkers, and strangers. The technique is named after the letters that make up the acronym. There are 4 prompts inside the FORM technique, that could let you discover new topics of communication to interrupt up awkward silences.

Family, Occupation, Recreation and Money are all a part of the acronym F.O.R.M. You can use those four topics to start a communique and examine greater approximately the person with whom you're speaking. Understanding this easy idea, you may be able to talk approximately topics of mutual hobby. On the entire, maximum human beings experience sharing stories approximately their lives with others. When you ask questions about them, they sense greater critical and it allows maintain the communique going. Let's take a closer look at the acronym:

F - Family. This subject matter makes a speciality of the opposite person's family. Questions to consider encompass the subsequent:

· Do you have any youngsters?

· Where did your circle of relatives or ancestors originate?

· How long have you ever been dwelling in this city? Then you may move into extra element and tell them approximately your personal stories.

O-Occupation. This subject matter makes a speciality of profession associated questions. Consider asking the following:

· What's your profession?

· What does it sense like to engage in that kind of paintings?

You and the opposite individual can examine notes on the similarities and variations among your respective positions.

R-Recreation. Ask them what they like to do for amusing whilst they're now not working. The high-quality way to get to know each different is to locate things you've got in commonplace. Consider asking them about their preferred pursuits or in the event that they experience sports.

M-Money. This entails non-non-public monetary topics. Inquire approximately their thoughts on current economic occasions. For instance, you may ask how did fuel expenses trade? Anything this is modern-day news and falls within impartial territory is honest sport for discussion. Keep in mind to keep away from personal questions like salaries and other touchy monetary topics.

In this chapter, you discovered how to make a primary affect and begin the initial levels of small talk conversation. In the following bankruptcy we are able to speak how to method small talk in a very not unusual tension-inducing environment-- business networking.

Chapter 12: Business Networking

Networking may be like going to the dentist for some human beings. When it involves attending enterprise events or contacting "the proper human beings," finding a prospect may be as nerve-wracking a root canal. However, in the process of finding a new task, small speak is often the key to beginning conversations and putting the stage for successful employment.

Despite the reality that networking has a terrible recognition, maximum people realize that it's far vital. Make your enjoy a bit much less painful via following these guidelines.

Creating connections

In order to get you up to the mark on how to make small speak be just right for you, I'd like to reframe the concept of networking. Rather than deliberating it as an pastime this is awesome out of your ordinary social interactions, don't forget networking as an extension of what you already do. Building relationships is all that networking is about.

Start a verbal exchange with industry colleagues or different people for your developing network by using imagining what you would say to a informal acquaintance or someone you have not seen in years. Get to recognise the person you are conversing with and display interest in them. There's no mystery formula to achieve networking. It's all about making connections with humans to your industry or an enterprise you'd like to work in, so you can research from every other.

Since small speak is regularly step one in establishing a rapport with a new acquaintance, don't move on a rant about yourself, your career dreams, or what you need from a ability companion.

A networking communication ought to begin by using asking questions. Firstly, it relieves you of the weight of having to give you some thing to mention; rather, you can honestly pay attention. The second reason is that it helps to interrupt the ice and begin the interaction.

Follow-up questions are a high-quality manner to expose you are listening and are inquisitive about what they have got to say. It is common to observe up a question approximately someone's direction to fulfillment with a question on how they found out about the industry, an exciting task, or their imaginative and prescient for the future of their profession.

Starting The Conversation

Many human beings discover the concept of starting a communication terrifying. When you spot a person throughout the room at a networking event or enterprise convention, whether or not or now not it's well worth introducing your self and gaining knowledge of them. Initiating a communique with a stranger does no longer should be as terrifying as it sounds. Begin with the aid of maintaining matters easy.

When it comes to networking occasions, it's unexpected how powerful it could be to honestly method a person and introduce your self or ask to sign up for their desk. It's also a very good idea to start a verbal exchange at the same time as waiting in line on the buffet desk. Observe the food and spot if you may begin an extended conversation with the aid of citing the issue. When you see them again, greet them and inquire approximately their revel in at the event.

During a networking occasion, you may inquire approximately someone's goals for the occasion, in addition to, who they assume might be an excellent creation. The reason you're on the event and the man or woman you're hoping to fulfill can be similar. This is an amazing opportunity to talk approximately your professional aspirations and the components of your process that you enjoy the most.

If you're having a assembly with a ability customer, convey up a subject that hasn't been discussed yet.

To alleviate some of the strain of keeping the communique going, it is a great idea to start asking questions once more. Good inquiries to ask encompass the subsequent:

·Is there whatever you've discovered in the beyond 12 months that has helped you the most?

·What do you think are the most urgent problems facing experts in our area?

·Over the past few years, how has automation changed the character of your work?

·Do you've got a favorite a part of working in or at a selected region or employer?

Talk about the news of the day.

It's constantly amusing to speak approximately the news, but remember to preserve it light. Vacation plans, new tech devices, and the weather are only some examples of subjects you can talk. Conversations may be difficult to keep away from while present day activities are especially contentious. Keep your thoughts to your self if the opposite individual raises a topic that would be controversial. Recognize and agree that the subject could be distressing, and then pass directly to lighter subjects of debate.

Don't convey up anything political or touchy to your conversation. Conversation, no longer soap boxing, is what you are trying to acquire.

As you may see from the furnished examples, there's no point out of you in any of them. That's all planned. Engaging others in verbal exchange approximately topics of hobby to them is the excellent manner to construct relationships. Let them inform you approximately themselves and their pursuits.

To avoid leaving the other man or woman with a vague affect of who you're, it's far essential to proportion a few private details about your self with them. You can take part inside the communication with the aid of expressing your very own thoughts on a given topic. Find areas in which you can believe them and relate your very own reports that are similar to what they're announcing. Discuss your professional aspirations. Keep your feedback to an affordable duration and recognition on the topic handy. Be keen to learn and to listen to what others have to mention. In the end, networking is all approximately expanding your horizons.

Occasionally, a stranger will arise to you and ask you a question. Try to keep away from giving one-word answers and provide you with a subject of conversation. Don't say "Fine" when someone asks, "How are you doing?" As simple because it sounds, begin the communique with the aid of announcing, "I'm nice. How are you?" The other character has something to reply to now, and you could comply with up with questions about their very own reports.

Small speak is a skill that may be honed over time. This may be implemented to a party or different social gatherings, as nicely. Maintaining recognition and energy at some stage in the communication may require some self-training in your component. Always make the effort to hold eye contact and display which you are inquisitive about what the opposite man or woman has to say.

Networking Icebreakers

Many human beings are afraid of coming near huge organizations of strangers whilst attending industry activities for the cause of constructing a professional community. In reality, you is probably awed by way of the ease with which some of your friends jump into these conditions. With a drink in hand, you might be the person that sits awkwardly by myself even as desperately seeking to come up with subjects to speak about.

However, with sufficient exercise you're much less probably to face out at those activities. In networking, I've discovered that the maximum vital a part of a successful communication is to have an icebreaker and a smooth ending declaration. If you're having trouble starting and ending conversations, attempt any of these icebreakers:

"Hi, how are you?" or "Hello, how's it going?"

This opener would possibly appear too not unusual, however it really works each single time. Icebreakers do not need to be difficult or complicated. Instead of treating the other individual merely as a prospective business touch, deal with them like the proper and real man or woman they're. Ask them about their day, in the event that they loved the beverages or snacks, give them a praise, or even better, ask them how they sense about the event itself. Ask "Why have you discovered yourself here?"

When you're trying to begin a communication, you shouldn't dig too deeply or too quick; as an alternative, you have to make small, regular steps into learning the other individual.

"What brings you right here?"

When breaking the ice, you need to chip away at it grade by grade, rather than digging too deep too quickly. By asking the other person why they got here to the event, you may examine greater about what they do and what their goals are. Once they answer this query, it is easy to invite greater questions which can be related to what they said.

"What are you doing these days?"

This communique starter gets the alternative character to speak more approximately their private and professional lives. Think of it as a greater thrilling manner to invite, "What do you do?" that doesn't force the man or woman to reply on a selected topic. Depending on in which you take the communication from there, you may find out what they do, wherein they paintings, and how much revel in they have.

"What are you currently running on that you're clearly enthusiastic about?"

When you ask a person approximately their favored ongoing initiatives, you can get a sense of what they care about. It also helps you to recognize them better on a expert and private level and examine more approximately their revel in and interests. You by no means recognize, perhaps you're both interested by the same matters.

"Do all people else here?"

This networking recreation facilitates you discover how comfortable the opposite person is at the occasion. When attending a networking occasion, a person who comes with a large organization of buddies or coworkers is probable to sense less tense than a person who attends the occasion on my own. If they do not know each person there, that is your danger to talk to them about paintings, and they will probably be glad you did. After you communicate, you can ask them to place you in contact with people they understand on the occasion.

"Where did you get your first activity?"

With this networking question, you are positive to get some thrilling solutions. Even even though that is a sincere question, you is probably greatly surprised to discover how diverse people started out their professional lives and where their paths ultimately led them.

"Have you ever met a superstar?"

This is a a laugh query that might cause you each talking approximately a funny movie star meeting or sighting in a random vicinity.

Look for a hazard to say something about them.

This very last item is extra of a suggestion than a question, even though it can elicit more than one answer. Employ your powers of observation to decide whether or not or not they may be wearing something exciting, including a t-blouse with sayings on it, or whether or now not they point out some thing you find fascinating. Use what you have observed to begin a verbal exchange, however don't be creepy approximately it so they do not get scared. This strategy requires a whole lot of tact. You cannot just leap in and talk to someone while they're in the center of some thing else.

I realize that sounds hard, however right here are some examples that you could trade and use:

· "Hello, if it is okay to say so, I love your jacket, shoes, bag, and outfit as a whole. You is probably able to deliver me some fashion recommendations."

· "Hello," I've been thinking about getting the same cellphone you've got. How do you like it?"

· "Hello, I could not assist however hear you assert something approximately topic X. Do you mind if I ask you a few questions on that?"

Once the ice is damaged, strive not to hold asking questions in the course of the conversation in order that it doesn't experience like a job interview or an interrogation. A good communicator will suggest that they are interested by what you have to mention and also will reply and tell stories. This manner, the whole lot is going easily and also you and the alternative character can enjoy the conversation.

Now is the time to inform the ones properly testimonies you've got been saving for a horrific day. In bankruptcy 7, you may discover ways to construct quick, enjoyable tales. You can talk whatever fascinating that you have either heard or visible. Just be cautious about what you inform human beings. Keep in thoughts, this isn't the moment to inform anybody approximately that vacation where you took jello shots and then woke up in a overseas county.

Finally, whilst it comes time to signal to the alternative individual which you want to deliver the communication to a near, transitional terms are your pleasant bet. Easy to keep in mind terms include:

·Have you got a card?

·"Seeing you once more was first-rate!"

·"It became excellent to talk to satisfy you."

·"In conclusion...

These "icebreakers" paintings in meetings and networking occasions, and if you use them right, they'll help you sense less frightened and keep away from making awkward small talk. If nothing else works, attempt giving a compliment. Everyone loves one.

Overall, the more you community, the simpler it's far to talk to human beings and make enterprise connections inside the destiny. In the subsequent chapter, I will speak how to have interaction with and understand the nuances of small talk in the workplace.

Chapter 13: Small Talk Office Etiquette

Sometimes it is no longer smooth to strike up a communique at paintings. Avoiding the awkward second of meeting a person and having no idea what to mention is one of the most commonplace reasons we keep away from eye touch, flip our heads away, and pretend to be on our phones.

Conversation starters like "howdy, what's up, how are you," or "how are you doing?" are assured to quit a conversation as soon as we muster the braveness to look them inside the eyes. Everyone is familiar with that these phrases are merely an try and be well mannered with out truely undertaking communication.

There are severa possibilities for socializing with coworkers at the office. Consider a few minutes earlier than the assembly starts offevolved, lunch, coffee breaks, or every other water cooler conversations that would arise.

For those moments of silence, you could fill them up with small talk. However, if you sincerely want to connect to your coworkers, you must have an insatiable interest approximately the alternative man or woman and their mind and emotions with regards to paintings.

Starting a communique, being curious approximately others, paying attention to what they've to mention, and making an effort to connect all take time and strength. There is nothing worthwhile in existence that is straightforward. Make positive you realize why those conversations are well worth having earlier than you talk what to speak about at work.

Conversations inside the workplace can be extremely powerful. Everywhere we look, we are able to locate interesting folks who can encourage, rejuvenate, unblock our wondering, and deliver our paintings lifestyles an extra layer of which means.

Finding a connection

Meeting new co-employees and locating not unusual ground can immediately liven up your workday.

It's the same thrill you get whilst you run right into a familiar face in a ordinary land. In the procedure of spending greater time and strength on the connection, you could develop a strong attachment to the man or woman with whom you have clicked and connected right now.

The new hyperlink will let you share thoughts and study from every other, boosting your professional lifestyles.

Unbiased wondering may be unlocked.

The handiest way you can trade the manner you notice others at work is to appearance past your personal prejudices and make an effort to understand what makes them tick.

While it is able to be tempting to attribute someone's bad conduct at paintings to a person flaw, it's essential to bear in mind the context in which they're behaving.

You may be able to better recognize your coworkers and associates if you method them with an open mind and a preference to examine, instead of resorting to a fight or flight reaction. It's possible for a difficult person to be extraordinarily cooperative whilst given the danger to provide an explanation for themselves.

The Best Ways to Strike up a Meaningful Conversation at Work

There are a few established methods to have productive conversations at work without resorting to small speak or making you experience self-aware.

The first method is to ask open-ended questions that elicit a response.

Self-merchandising is a fave hobby for lots. It is possible to begin a verbal exchange by way of asking a query that is each curious approximately the individual and their work.

A person needs to be affirmed, understood, and valued so one can survive psychologically. Empathy is like a breath of fresh air for the character you're paying attention to. Following the fulfillment of this essential requirement, you can then focus on influencing or solving troubles. Some simple open-ended questions for the office consist of the subsequent:

· Have you deliberate any journeys for this year?

· Have you lately read any right books?

· Have you deliberate whatever fun for this weekend?

· How was the morning traffic?

· How long does your each day journey to paintings take?

· What are you having for lunch?

Listen extra and speak less.

Talking and listening need to be balanced so as for a conversation to achieve success. The best manner to talk and shape a reference to another character is thru energetic listening, even supposing it's miles tough. Aspiring conversationalists have to practice paying attention. Projecting authentic interest is the only way to make your self stand out. Inquire approximately matters that others will discover thrilling and fun to talk about.

It's crucial which you ask the proper inquiries to get the communique commenced, so that you can study greater about the individual you are talking with. It's smooth for others to inform whilst we're simply pretending to be fascinated.

Avoid adopting a sufferer mentality.

A communication need to no longer start with a bad evaluation of a person or some thing, inclusive of "Our boss sucks" or "This presentation is a waste of time."

Even in case you think the opposite character feels the equal, approaching a verbal exchange with a victim angle is a terrible idea. When you whinge all the time, you return out as a crybaby and deny the opposite man or woman an opportunity to talk. When you technique others with a terrible attitude, you also run the danger of alienating them and causing them to keep away from you within the future.

Your conversation can be remembered for the feelings it inspires, so it is vital to ask questions which might be uplifting. Try to invite questions a good way to make you experience top. As a questioner, you can affect the path of the conversation by asking the right ones. Find topics to discuss with the alternative person so one can advantage both of your private lives.

Recognize and admire your non-public obstacles.

When it involves talking and sharing, one of a kind people have various degrees of comfort. You should have the ability to inform whilst a query is getting too non-public or inflicting soreness for the opposite person.

It's also important to notice that disagreeing with someone is not similar to bullying them.

Disagree, however do so in a manner that does not stumble upon as non-public.

When you assert, "I do not agree with that...," the other man or woman becomes shielding. Instead of disagreeing, ask, "Tell me why you think this..." They'll be greater receptive. You can also say, "I have special opinion on the matter. Would you want to percentage your mind?"

Accept the fact which you aren't invincible.

Many behavioralists trust that we must grow to be at risk of permit others to see us and make significant connections.

The truth is, while we don't know some thing, we are embarrassed to admit it, so we pretend to be informed and nod in agreement rather than showing genuine hobby in gaining knowledge of more. Having a superficial communication is needless if you want to establish a relationship based on mutual recognize and accept as true with.

Be your self and don't fake to be someone or recognize some thing you don't. Accept your ignorance and say, "Oh, I'm no longer sure" while a topic comes up that you lack understanding in.

Vulnerability is the important thing to beginning a communication and developing a long-lasting relationship.

Simply stating "I don't know a good deal about XYZ" can get the ball rolling when you preserve with the aid of asking "How about if I pick out your brain to find out greater?"

Always maintain it easy.

Our minds get slowed down in looking to give you the suitable question, and we turn out to be giving up at the concept of speaking to someone because we can not discover one.

It does not always necessitate a ideal start to a conversation. Get started out somewhere and then set a route for the rest of it. You can get the communique going by means of definitely asking the subsequent questions when you have not anything else to say:

·In what approaches do you experience your paintings?

·What do you do for a laugh?

·What are you currently gaining knowledge of?

·Who is the maximum influential man or woman for your life?

·What techniques do you use to live on pinnacle of your recreation?

·What new talents are you operating on?

·I'm interested by learning greater approximately XYZ. Where can one locate extra information in this subject matter?

The maximum important element to take into account is to stay within the second. The warfare among human connection over a digital one is becoming more and more difficult in brand new global of constant distractions. However, if we are continuously preoccupied, we're not adding some thing to the conversation. We have to be completely present in order to have an amazing communique.

Rather than permitting yourself to be distracted, start a communication through pledging to be absolutely gift. Make eye contact with the person sitting subsequent to you instead of staring at your cellular cellphone all of the time. If we can learn to hook up with all of the interesting people in our work surroundings, we will have a better enjoy at paintings. In interactions that go past casual communicate, the preference to research from each other can be a terrific source of strength.

Do's and Don'ts

If you're in a commercial enterprise placing, you are much more likely to be chatting with your co-employees than you are together with your friends. Unlike small talk, there's a cause to the chit-chat, which will be to community or study extra approximately your customers.

For one component, you will often have the ability to plot ahead of time for social occasions. You can, for instance, use social networks like LinkedIn to discover more approximately your conference attendees. Conversation subjects can be based totally on the pursuits and interests indexed of their profile.

Many groups and businesses have established regulations about what's and isn't proper place of work verbal exchange. There are many unwritten guidelines of business verbal exchange, and it could be tough to know which topics to keep away from.

Never begin a verbal exchange with the hard promote in case you're networking to sell your service or product. The more you learn about the alternative person, the much more likely it is that you may have a nice courting with them.

When discussing the climate, human beings are generally happy to achieve this, even though it looks like an overused topic of conversation before everything. It is completely non-offensive and permits anyone to express themselves. A easy query is the very best approach to start a communication.

Start by locating out how long they've worked of their cutting-edge position or how they got into their selected profession course. As cited, by no means begin a communication with a business request or a hard promote; as a substitute, show hobby in the different person and ask questions.

Many people experience discussing their travel plans, in which they had been and what their next destination might be. The communication will begin to flow if you show hobby.

You can also start a verbal exchange with a reference to the maximum current should-watch drama or fact display. Often called "water-cooler topics," those subjects of conversation are what people talk approximately when they accumulate around the water cooler within the workplace.

Likewise, you can never go incorrect with meals. You can start the communication by using inquiring about human beings's favorite local restaurants, bars, or street food vendors and then requesting their recommendation.

Use social media to live updated on what is happening for your local location – it is one of the nice ways to stay knowledgeable. A few good starters are "What do you consider the schools ultimate because of the snow?" and "Have you heard about the new improvement out-of-city?" This particular topic has the benefit of creating you appear informed and engaged in local affairs. This can be some thing you both currently attended, or it may be an event which you've simply heard approximately. Remember to listen extra than you communicate.

You can use the following subjects for small speak within the office:

·Local sporting occasions, especially if the team is having a a success season

·Recent popular activities just like the Super Bowl, the Oscars, and the Grammys.

·Netflix, Amazon, and popular tv suggests

·If it's Friday and you're looking for activities within the region, this is a additionally exact location to start.

·Long weekends and essential vacations, specifically when they're nearing.

·Preparations for destiny holidays, in particular if it's miles excessive season like the summer time or school breaks. Likewise, in case you understand they have got these days again from a weekend or excursion, inquire about their journey.

·A compliment on a chunk of garb or an accent is powerful even if it is a minor hairstyle trade.

·Cool apps or beneficial web sites, in particular if they help you do paintings higher.

Topics to Avoid

The following listing of topics should be averted in any respect costs:

· It's pleasant to avoid speaking about cash or whatever monetary, such as salaries or bonuses. It's feasible that speaking about the housing marketplace and what sort of a person spent for his or her most current domestic is taboo in a few groups.

· The dialogue of political issues can often deliver people pretty a long way apart. If you do not refrain from taking part in the dialogue, you face the danger of frightening or separating at least one of the other people inside the room. It's satisfactory to avoid topics around religion with strangers as it's a private count number that many humans have strong evaluations about.

· If you have these days misplaced a cherished one, had a health scare, or have an extended-time period health trouble, don't carry it up in verbal exchange. In the presence of strangers, keep away from topics like these that might potentially be upsetting.

· When it involves someone's look or age, avoid making personal feedback. In order to be successful at small talk, it is vital to keep away from making the opposite person sense self-conscious even in case you think you're complimenting them.

In this section, you have got found out the way to interact in small talk with those you figure around. In the following bankruptcy, we will take a broader step back where you will discover ways to initiate small communicate to create a communique that is each memorable and fun for the other individual.

Chapter 14: Creating A Conversation Of Substance

A communication is maximum profitable while it facilitates you gain a higher know-how of yourself, the other man or woman, or the sector. We should well known that small speak is critical to our properly-being and ought to now not be painful, but meaningful verbal exchange stays an extended manner off. This is the sort of verbal exchange in which we depart the shallows of pleasantries in the back of and dive deeper.

Because of our innate want to express ourselves, we discover meaning in gaining knowledge of ourselves. Self-expression is the primary of three elements which could make a communique in reality treasured, in step with social psychologist Kirsty Gardiner on the University of East London. For the maximum part, we yearn for the danger to talk our minds and move in addition into the subjects that count number maximum to us. In order to feel understood, we need to be capable of explicit what we sense in phrases and proportion them with someone who can validate them. If we need to have a definitely meaningful communique, we need someone to pay attention to us. A properly listener allows us to see ourselves thru the eyes of the person we're talking with.

Also important for a meaningful communique according to Gardiner, is the ability to better apprehend oneself.

Even although maximum folks want to have a deeper communication, many people aren't appropriate at actively listening or bridging the communique in order that both events can take part in an integrated manner.

The speaker and the listener both have a function in a -manner communication. While being attentive to what the opposite individual has to say about themselves, we get a hazard to examine greater approximately who they are as people. Meaningful conversations educate us about ourselves, others, and the arena. When this occurs, we ultimately sense better understood and related to those round us. You can use the subsequent concepts to improve the content material of your conversations:

Don't get too excited about the next concept you've got in mind.

When you are now not paying interest, people note due to the fact you are usually considering some thing else. With their flip is over, don't be eager to inform them about an wonderful experience you had. You ought to constantly listen before you communicate. If the story you want to inform is interesting, it's going to nevertheless be engaging five minute from now.

Show your interest in a subject by asking correct questions.

Showing proper interest in what the other individual has to mention is a brilliant manner to demonstrate that you're paying interest. At least one question have to be asked earlier than shifting on to the subsequent issue. This will make it less complicated for you to connect to the other person or find a way in which you can assist them.

Do your homework in a non-creepy way.

Preparing yourself for a communique is one factor; being creepy is some other. Look on the character's social money owed before you start a deliberate conversation to get a feel of their professional lifestyles and hobbies. Having a higher information of a person offers you a leg up at the opposition. You'll have the ability to connect with them more without difficulty, and you could avoid awkward conversations.

Don't be afraid to assist others.

You need to usually inquire about how you can be of carrier to the human beings you meet. Despite what you watched, they realize what's best for them. There are so many chances to meet new human beings and build relationships while you understand what your target market values most.

You will stick out from the gang if all you do is lend a supporting hand. Only a small percentage of people who make a promise to help others really keep their quit of the good buy. To benefit the believe of others, you need to offer them with exactly what they asked: a touch, a device, or a sounding board.

Don't brag approximately how notable you are all the time.

The fine human beings don't need to brag approximately how top notch they're to every person they meet. As the communique progresses, people will obviously begin to regard you as a hero.

Recognize the faces of others.

If you ever locate your self in a state of affairs wherein you may be surrounded by means of a variety of human beings, evaluate these principles again. The extra you reflect onconsideration on those thoughts, the much more likely you are to put them into exercise. If you follow those suggestions, you may see much less wasted time and extra probabilities to examine new matters from normal conversations.

Understanding Conversational Flow

Flow in a communique means that the entirety appears to move easily whilst you're speaking to a person. With go with the flow, you frequently do not feel anxious or awkward. You're never trapped, and you could solution and concentrate as if the conversation had been a dance. But every conversation is exclusive due to the fact there are numerous things that may exchange how you sense as you talk to the alternative individual. With this being said, glide can once in a while seem hard to acquire. However, with exercise, you can become very good at growing glide in maximum conversations, similar to you may with many other conversational abilties.

Flow is most probably to manifest while matters feel clean. With some people, we just get in conjunction with the manner they're and the way they communicate. In those conditions, we feel like we simply linked with the person we were speaking to because we shared information or, in private situations, feelings. To enhance our communique competencies, we will observe what we've discovered right here. The first degree is to recollect a person with whom you struck up an instantaneous rapport. You failed to must work hard to get the communique going; it just went, and you didn't even recognise how you came up with the words or questions you used. Once you've got a person in thoughts, there are a few steps you can take to determine out what made this communication glide. Ask your self the subsequent:

· What had been this man or woman's qualities?

· Who were given the communique going?

· What did I say whilst we had been speakme?

· What induced the interaction?

· How lengthy did this interplay remaining?

· What did the opposite man or woman say?

·

Situational elements are also critical. Timing is while the verbal exchange occurred, like what time of day, what time of year, or if it happened at a vacation celebration or at work.

Consider asking yourself the subsequent:

· When did it show up?

· Where did it take place?

These are essential considering that they provide suggestions as to how you would possibly organically build float. Each of those questions will give you a clearer photograph of the specific situations of this conversation and this person, with a purpose to assist you discern out why the communication went so properly.

It might appear like quite a few paintings to break down and examine a communique on this manner, but doing so permit you to analyze loads about your natural capability to make communication glide. The subsequent level on this method might be to remember a situation and someone with whom you had a communication that became especially difficult to navigate. To put it some other manner, you did not make any progress inside the interplay. Ask your self the identical questions you did to find the perfect glide of an interplay. One manner to do those physical games is to jot down them next to each other on a piece of paper. When you are completed, examine the two gadgets. Do you see any ordinary thoughts? In order to avoid overthinking or overanalyzing the data you got here up with, write down the primary mind that spring to thoughts. It's frequently true to write down what you're considering after completing a self-discovery hobby, consisting of writing down what you've been mulling over.

Once you have a better concept of ways your personal conversations drift or don't glide, it may be helpful to reflect onconsideration on the extra large factors that affect the waft of any interplay. No interactions are the same, but you can beautify your capability to seamlessly have interaction in small chat by specializing in a few commonplace matters about how talks waft. For producing float, all you want to recognise is to "preserve the person speaking." However, it's viable that the alternative individual is speaking so much that it is tough so one can reply. As a result, communique may additionally end up stuttering. But in awkward conversations where you sense like you will never get the waft going, it could be beneficial to just get the opposite individual to speak.

Think about when you talk the maximum. It's in all likelihood when you're talking about some thing you care approximately or are excited about. Asking smart questions may reveal what the man or woman cares about even if you do not know them at all. This is vital statistics because if you sense just like the verbal exchange isn't going everywhere, you may use what is important to that individual to get it going again. Some signs that a person cares approximately a topic are when they change their tone or use greater expression of their voice, maintain speaking approximately that subject matter, or display emotion via their phrases or facial expressions. Keep those essential topics in thoughts, and because the communication goes on, convey them up via asking a question. This shows that you are listening and care about the person while additionally encouraging them to speak greater.

Next, you need to care approximately the individual you are speaking to for the restrained time you've got with them. If humans are sincere with themselves, they'll admit that this isn't always smooth. There are a few human beings we just don't get in conjunction with. This might be because we've got a awful first impact of them or due to the fact they offend us in some manner.

For the constrained period of time you've got with that character, it is less complicated to hold the communique going if there may be a purpose to care about them. If you do not connect with someone, it's difficult to care approximately what's crucial to them, and it's often in those varieties of conversations that we can not make the communique waft. If you observed you is probably feeling this way, make a personal inquiry. Ask your self, "What is it about this character that rubs me the incorrect manner?" This will help you preserve an open mind during the communique, due to the fact as quickly as you start to experience annoyed, irritated, or shielding, you may close down and the conversation will give up. This may be difficult to do at paintings due to the fact the person may be capable of assist you with a venture or play a important role for your professional development. So, retaining an open thoughts is an vital manner to hold a verbal exchange going and try to get it to glide. Remember that they have a beyond and reviews that may affect how they communicate or act, and that your verbal exchange with them could not only help you, however additionally have an effect on their life.

Getting to understand the alternative character and displaying that you care will make each of you sense extra comfortable. With a little bit of comfort at the start, flow has a chance to take place. Conversational drift is all about ensuring that you and the opposite individual have an equal amount of time to talk approximately yourself and to percentage records. So hold song of the time. Do you ever experience like you're speaking for a long time? If so, ask the man or woman to come back back in and proportion their opinion. To carry a person again into the conversation, you may make open-ended statements, which could take the form of questions.

A properly instance of that is while someone wants to recognize, "How became the presentation?" If you stated, "It went first-rate," the communication would be over. If you need to have a longer, more significant conversation with that character, you have to say some thing like, "I assume it became a achievement. I worked in A, B and C. Is there whatever else I could have included?" This encourages the alternative individual to respond, preserving the speak going. However, in case your number one cause with that man or woman is to develop your professional network or searching for advancement, you need to make each effort feasible to keep an open communicate. The more details you deliver on your solution, the more you can invite the other man or woman to answer as nicely. It's like giving the ball to someone else in a basketball recreation. The ball need to move backward and forward in a way that sounds herbal.

Small Talk Transitioning

The capacity to transport from small speak to the subject you actually need to speak about is an often-left out ability. Transitions aren't only for writing; they are additionally crucial while speaking. Given that Americans are aware of small talk earlier than they start discussing the reason in their meeting or appointment, that is even extra genuine. As a be counted of truth, most individuals recall it disrespectful to forgo the small talk altogether. As a result, how can we get beyond small communication to what you really want to speak approximately?

If you're trying to pass from small talk to the actual purpose you initiated a verbal exchange, or in case you just want to change the topic of conversation for any reason, right here are some critical transitions that speakers make.

· In addition...

· That makes me think of...

· In mild of this, allow me just say...

· Before I lose my reminiscence...

· While I'm contemplating it...

· I absolutely got here up with an idea.

· Oh, there may be one more component I'd like to say (or ask you about).

· This is unrelated to what we are discussing, yet...

· For a moment, I'd need to shift gears...

· Weirdly, we've got experienced something similar.

(Remember, it's not important for it to be a laugh. A extra common manner to use this phrase is to mention, "That's fascinating, due to the fact I experienced some thing comparable as soon as."

· In any case, I understand this isn't always absolutely relevant, however...

· I realise that is a diversion, but...

After you have correctly made transitions in the conversation, you must experience more confident and in control. It is critical, however, to no longer misguide the communique in an uncomfortable direction.

Taking Control of the Conversation

You have a whole lot of influence whilst you know how to begin a dialogue. However, this newfound authority have to lead to a deeper awareness of your own identification. "Control" can be a strong phrase whilst we speak about being in charge of a discourse. In this context, having control does now not mean instructing others what to do or shouting over them. In truth, the goal of controlling the communication's framing is to get the opposite character involved as an awful lot as viable. Frame your phrases so that it piques the interest of the listener, now not so that you can impose your personal thoughts or ideals on them.

In order to begin a verbal exchange, you ought to first pick out the meant target market. Do you understand this character? If that is the case, how did you first stumble upon them? What do you believe you studied in their listening capabilities? Do they appear to be effortlessly irritated? Is it clean for them to get bored or neglect what you said while you're talking to them?

These questions have to be requested of yourself before you begin a verbal exchange with every other character. At paintings, where you can have scheduled meetings, that is simpler to perform. However, you by no means understand whilst a risk come upon can bring you collectively with a person who let you amplify your professional network. Think approximately what you wish to advantage from this speak that became no longer a part of your plan. This man or woman has the capacity to help you advance for your profession. Perhaps your goal is to expose off your very own capabilities or reviews whilst simultaneously demonstrating an interest on this man or woman's work by means of structuring the query. Asking questions to examine extra approximately the opposite individual's pastimes and employment will let you steer the communique within the proper course. However, you may assume that not every person will reply to your inquiries. Validation and redirection abilties are essential in this situation. A dialogue can be controlled by means of taking a brief have a look at what you want to get out of it and using that to come up with questions which carry the communication to that cease.

You'll be able to weave together the conversation's framework with this potential, which entails validating and then redirecting. Try to carry up a specific difficulty or subject in a verbal exchange by using asking questions or making assertions. However, the verbal exchange may be interrupted by way of the alternative man or woman's tries to trade the issue or snatch the reins of the verbal exchange. Avoiding paying attention to what they have to mention may want to pop out as disrespectful, uninterested, or rude. In this example, verification is crucial. A courteous but direct approach to carry the other individual lower back to what you were discussing is to say some thing like, "Yes, I can see why this is, John," after which observe up through pointing out, "But what did you watched of my point concerning X?" Essentially, it shows that you were aware of what the opposite man or woman turned into saying even as also expressing an hobby in what that they had to mention in return. Bring up something they stated earlier inside the communique and spot if you can tie it to some thing you need to mention later in the discussion. If you are nevertheless listening, it way you are nonetheless interested by what they have got to mention. In this manner, it'll show which you were listening and paying attention. To create a operating partnership, you may carry up that topic over and over in the course of the discussion. In the end, it's still up to you to decide how the conversation progresses.

Always Read The Other Person

A communication can be difficult for the alternative individual because of the manner you technique it. Keeping an eye fixed on the alternative person's feelings and reactions is vital on this scenario. You have to be capable of read the other character so as to body a communicate. Being in rate of the communique method that you are answerable for ensuring the alternative individual is okay. You may be the who's leading the communication, but does the alternative person's expression display that she or he failed to like some thing you said? Try to keep away from searching at them in the event that they seem apprehensive or try and cover their face. In this case, it can be that you're speaking about a subject that the person is unfamiliar with or has previously had negative reports with. You'll need to expose the alternative individual that you care approximately them in these eventualities. Saying some thing like, "I observed you appear a little dissatisfied via this. If you ever need to talk, let me recognise," in a expert context can be appropriate due to the fact you'll be in a position to tell how the other person responds to your phrases.

The pleasant path of action in this example is to be open and sincere with the person you're talking to about your observations, however achieve this with compassion and know-how. While this talk might also deviate from the topic to hand, you're capable of take in expertise and determine what to do with it even when the concern is no longer applicable in your targets. This is the simplest form of framing.

Always pay attention to how the alternative character responds while discussing difficult topics or whilst they arrive up in communique. Don't disregard any signs which you're getting a reaction. People might also see you negatively because of this. However, actual assist and sympathy are the best methods to have interaction with every other. If the talk you're having now isn't always the best second to have it, then it's important which you come to be privy to this and alter the subject of communication therefore. As a end result, framing is much less about taking manage of a dialogue. It is greater about using your communique abilties to proportion and obtain statistics in methods that make the conversation what it wishes to be at that specific region, time, and with that particular individual.

The Art of Framing

You can use the artwork of framing to study how to cope with any scenario that comes up in communication and nevertheless feel like you've got performed some thing, whether or not it's giving assist or getting statistics or creating a connection or receiving acclaim for your plan.

It's crucial to keep enhancing your own self-recognition as you continue to exercise the many aspects of framing a verbal exchange. To begin a communique, it is important to be self-conscious, which involves distinguishing between your beliefs and what you genuinely recognize. Discerning this difference can have a sizeable effect on how you method a communication. When discussing a challenge at work, it's important to paste to the records so as to provide a specific timeline of the challenge's development. In what order did the whole thing move from begin to finish? Consider your personal feelings approximately the group individuals you've got labored with, as well as the events that have taken location all through the route of the undertaking. Keep in thoughts, even though, the purpose of your discussion and the way your framing aids in attaining that intention always. So, in case your factor of view doesn't add anything to the discussion, it should not be added up. The ability to be self-conscious is critical in this ability set, as you can unwittingly deliver up a topic or scenario that is out of context. When you discover that you've long past off on a tangent, the other person "assessments out", and you've overlooked the opportunity to explicit what you needed to mention.

Make a factor of paying close attention to the words you use, as well as the words used by others. I think this is a superb method to border the dialogue. The capacity to pick out the proper words to use in a given scenario is an critical one to master. Language is like paint on a portray; how you use it'll have an impact at the flow of the communication. Observing your self in verbal exchange might assist you figure out wherein you're currently in phrases of the language you use. When describing an event, a task, or a person else, be aware of the words you operate. Is there a habitual topic? Is it common so as to transfer up your vocabulary depending at the context? Is it viable which you use unique terms depending in your temper? It's tough to preserve song of all the many methods words can be located collectively.

There is no doubt that words can also have a profound effect at the manner we see the world around us. It's smooth to look how words we use affect our lives without us even spotting it via media and advertising. Ads and headlines hire a whole lot of word choices to elicit a selected reaction from us. For quite a few human beings, the power of phrases comes from their ability to influence people's feelings. By evoking a specific emotion or notion in every other individual, you could improve the pleasant of your interactions with that individual. Keeping in thoughts, even though, what I spoke earlier about how being gift permits you to peer the opposite man or woman. It is your obligation as the one leading the speak to respond with compassion in case you purpose someone else to enjoy something they are unable to endure.

Remembering the impact words have on a communique, it turns into clean that the phrases you choose can influence the entire course of a dialogue.

It's also a good idea to look what the character's move-to terms and words are. Depending at the situation, this records can help you get the verbal exchange started out or permit you to return in your authentic frame of reference. There are instances, even though, whilst it is able to be useful to include a number of the other person's phrases or terms into your very own communication. Counselors frequently appoint this method at the same time as running with customers. Therapy may be greater effective if it consists of the purchaser's mind and emotions into the technique. To ensure that their goals are reached, therapists set the tone for every session, however they can preserve their clients engaged with the aid of the use of the other individual's phrases.

A awesome deal of have an effect on may be won by studying the artwork of conversation structuring. The most essential factor to keep in thoughts while growing those competencies is to consider what you need out of the communication and make certain you aren't putting in a one-sided discussion. Even while you want the alternative character to walk away with something, you need to also be aware of what they say and the way they are saying it (even non-verbally). It's no longer approximately being in command; it is about taking control of the discussion. The potential to recognize when the verbal exchange desires to be rebalanced a good way to make the alternative character feel crucial and took part is a crucial part of both large and small speak communication.

Here are a few key takeaways from this bankruptcy:

Keep an open mind and act as an observer. Every time you have interaction with every other person, you're sending a message. They're proper in the front people, but we do not see them most of the time. Pay attention to nonverbal cues, which include frame language, tone of voice, and emotional outbursts, as well as verbal cues. Reading body language provides you the advantage of being capable of efficaciously control a conversation.

Observe your thoughts. Try to be greater conscious of what you are displaying people whilst they're performing in ways that do not mesh with the conversation or what they are announcing. Even the manner someone responds to us might be a reflect of our moves. It's viable to tell if their conduct is a result of your actions through listening to what you are doing. Your behavior is a mirrored image of what they may be wondering and feeling in case you treat them with appreciate.

Understand which you have manage over the path of a discussion thru the questions you ask and the answers you provide. Respect and expertise are fostered through asking considerate questions and paying near attention to the responses you receive. It's clean to say, "I have a extraordinary point of view. Would you concentrate to me and then inform me what you think?" More in all likelihood than not, the alternative individual will concentrate to you if you listened to them first.

Maintain a degree head. We've all had a few heated debates in the past. Take it in stride while others express their displeasure. Try to decipher what those phrases characterize with the aid of asking further questions.

Listen to what the other person has to say and attempt to understand what they are announcing. As a end result, the verbal exchange becomes more rational and less irrational.

Honesty is key. A discussion can become stale if you do not make the effort to understand the opposite individual. You must time table a time while you can dedicate your whole awareness to them if you can not deliver them your full attention proper now. Genuine hobby in knowledge and gaining knowledge of is the source of sincerity. A loss of sincerity can cause human beings mistaking you for a manipulator.

An effective discussion starts with an awareness of the communique's natural float. When beginning, you have to confirm the path in which it'll go. In order to do that, you should be willing to leap in. Once you're within the go with the flow, there are a lot of things you could do that can both maintain you there and help you get there. If you are inclined to put within the effort and time, you may reap the rewards.

We have discussed plenty on this chapter about growing a fascinating communication and directing it in the direction of a high-quality outcome. In the following chapter, you'll learn how to each shape and produce exciting anecdotes.

Chapter 15: Telling Stories

I'll be the primary to admit that small talk may be extremely tedious. Yes, it's far a extensively recounted professional courtesy, however you and I both realize that it regularly involves being attentive to a reputedly endless series of horribly banal anecdotes.

But, regrettably, we all experience the unavoidable stress to fill that awkward silence, which leads inside the occasional utterance of, nicely, much less-than-exciting anecdotes. Nonetheless, it doesn't want to be this manner. There are ideas you ought to internalize to make even the dullest, maximum tedious, snore-inducing story barely extra engaging.

Small Talk Storytelling Structure

1. Tell stories that fit the environment and setting.

You should handiest proportion tales which are relevant to the modern-day topic and mood of a conversation. In other phrases, if you're having a effective speak with someone, inform joyful tales. If the temper is extra extreme, tell unhappy tales; and so on. It does not be counted how top notch a story is that if it does not match the context or the surroundings.

Be positive to listen to what the alternative individual has to mention. Don't hold speaking approximately your narrative if the challenge shifts.

2. Stay faraway from testimonies in that you are the hero.

A story about a war is almost constantly extra interesting than a tale about winning. Success is often more interesting whilst it comes after a fight. This is why "rags to riches" storylines are so famous in films, tv, and books.

Speaking nicely of your self remains an choice. You don't should make a laugh of your self all of the time. However, your target market is not likely to be enthralled by a story that focuses solely in your nice tendencies or achievements.

three. Make sure you tell the right narrative to the proper character.

In preferred, in case your target audience can relate to the tale considering they've been in a comparable situation, they will in all likelihood revel in it. If so, they may discover the narrative more a laugh because they are able to pick out with it.

Consider your audience's information and heritage when getting ready your content. Avoid the use of jargon or technical terms until your audience has some familiarity with your subject and industry.

You ought to additionally recall what topics and types of comedy your audience likes or doesn't like. Your grandparents might not be inquisitive about listening to about what you probably did after a night of ingesting, however it is able to work well in an casual amassing of friends.

4. Don't provide away the finishing in the beginning of a tale.

The first-rate tales start at the lowest. First, you acquire a feel of the context and the history of the scenario. In order to hold the listener's attention, you provide additional information earlier than eventually giving the punch line.

five. Start your tale with a sturdy hook.

You need to start a tale with a hook rather than plunging proper into it. The cause of a hook isn't to present away the plot of your narrative, but to lure the reader with a memorable anecdote. It is crucial to narrate the tale from the bottom up, but the hook have to now not betray the ending.

6. Do no longer attempt to outdo the tales of others.

When a tale is well obtained, it is clean to consider other memories we ought to tell. We clearly hope to elicit the equal kind of response from others as the individual who simply received it. On the other hand, if we without delay start talking approximately our personal reports, the alternative character may additionally experience undercut or dethroned. This takes their highlight away.

An a laugh story about the other man or woman's time in Spain might also lead you to keep away from citing some thing a whole lot funnier that came about to you while you were there.

However, you need to avoid tales that make different humans feel insufficient.

7. The plot must be based logically.

A tale should have a beginning, a middle, and a end to be able to be comprehensible. The tale as a whole should not cross on for extra than a couple of minutes, as a preferred rule.

Avoid going lower back to an earlier a part of the tale just to ensure you failed to miss some thing vital. Interruptions can be prevented with the aid of pronouncing, "Hold that belief, it is an entire different story!" and persevering with on.

eight. Establish the story with just sufficient element.

There are those who can move on and on approximately the trivia of a narrative for hours, however in no way get to the point of the story itself. As a end result, their audience will become disinterested. Setting the placing necessitates a bit of historical past information, however it should now not overwhelm the reader with specifics. It's hard to understand the message of a story when the context is ignored.

What passed off the night time earlier than is beside the point to the tale you are trying to carry, so don't carry it up. Your listeners might be puzzled in case you don't make it clean to them that your story came about within the morning.

nine. Be innovative together with your word selections.

Using some vivid descriptions in your story can help keep your target market engaged, however overdoing it is able to come off as over-the-top.

10. Make the narrative come to life through using your voice.

Listeners may discover it hard to pay attention even in case your narrative is fun if you speak in a humdrum manner. A listeners' attention is held by using the best of the storyteller's voice. The quantity, pitch and tone of your voice may be adjusted by experimenting with those components. When describing thrilling activities on your tale, communicate faster to bring a experience of urgency and depth. When you want to emphasise a specific moment or turn within the narrative, you ought to use a louder voice.

Create a awesome "voice" for each man or woman to your story, without making them into caricatures. If you operate this an excessive amount of, your target market turns into disengaged from the tale.

eleven. Make eye touch with your audience.

According to popular notion, one have to be able to appearance a person in the attention even as telling the reality. It is generally inferred that people who are not able to hold eye contact are hiding something. Using good enough eye touch permit you to encounter as more dependable, attractive, and sincere for your communique with the audience.

12. Make use of gestures to help illustrate your point.

When telling a story, gestures are a first rate tool. This is an powerful manner to get your audience's imaginations working for you. Gestures can decorate your public speakme skills, as a manner of expressing enthusiasm. It is viable to appoint lots of gestures whilst offering a tale, which includes:

· Moving your arms aside or closer collectively, to bring distance or item size.

· Lifting or decrease your hand together with your palm facing down to signify the peak of a person or thing.

· Shrugging and raising each hands skyward to convey resignation or depression.

13. Pauses could make a scene greater dramatic.

It's feasible to add anxiety, intrigue, and clarity for your storytelling by means of using brief pauses to break the waft of your narrative.

14. Express yourself thru your face.

You can make your story extra thrilling with the aid of using your face to specific your feelings. Doing this in the front of the replicate may help you find out how certain emotions experience, specifically in case you're now not specifically expressive yourself.

How To Avoid Bad Storytelling

It's uncomfortable while you inform a story and get no response. In order to avoid this, you should discover ways to maintain every person's attention and convert mundane happenings into thrilling tales. Rather than leaping into an anecdote simply to make a factor, don't forget the subsequent: if someone else were to inform you this story, might you locate it even remotely thrilling?

Keep the subsequent tips in mind whilst telling testimonies in a small talk putting.

Always Be Prepared

The sincere fact is that the majority of human beings do not don't forget their personal small communicate testimonies to be particularly fascinating, honestly due to the fact they are now not engaging in story-telling themselves. As well mannered as it is, responding to a traditional inquiry along with "How changed into your day?" with "It went nicely, how was yours?" does not exactly qualify as a captivating narrative.

Being organized with a narrative that you could amplify on will be beneficial, even though it isn't always a moving monologue that might be great complemented by means of a complete string orchestra.

It doesn't depend what you probably did in the course of the day; the point is to locate something that has a clear starting, middle, and cease that merits various brief, half-hearted words.

Don't Ramble

Let's face it, whilst telling testimonies, lots of us clumsily ramble on and lose tune of the principle factor. After stumbling our manner thru a slew of filler phrases and in reality superfluous information, we subsequently kind of, type of, almost make it to the most exciting part of the story.

Whether you are sharing an revel in at a networking occasion, in a activity interview, or certainly with a expert pal you took place to run into, attempt your exceptional to cut via the rambling and get to the coronary heart and soul of your tale. It will increase the level of engagement amongst your audience.

Discover Some Areas of Agreement

Have you ever had a coworker force you to take a seat down and examine all of their holiday photographs from a current trip? There's a terrific chance you have been bored to tears. Even if it sounds harsh, human nature dictates that we've got exceedingly little interest in matters that do not without delay pertain to ourselves.

Choosing an anecdote that is applicable to each of you is the best way to ensure that your conversational accomplice is completely engaged in something narrative you're telling them.

Speaking about something that at least slightly resonates along with your conversational companion will assist to keep his or her hobby, even if your narrative itself is not particularly compelling.

Don't Skimp at the Finer Points

When relaying a tale, you is probably tempted to cut out all of the details which are concerned. And, yes, they could come off as a bit flowery and superfluous at times—and you honestly don't need to ramble on for an eternity in an try to absolutely describe some thing that is completely beside the point.

It's vital to consider, although, that a few specifics also are what gives your story a touch lifestyles and appeal. As a result, withstand the temptation to cast off them all at once.

Consider this: Would you be interested by being attentive to a tale in which the scene turned into in no way established and all adjectives had been eliminated? Most probable, now not. Leaving out the bit approximately how involved you have been earlier than that presentation makes your narrative approximately giving that presentation much less memorable.

In different words, while you do not need to bore your readers with the insignificant details of your story, don't be afraid to be a bit theatrical and descriptive that allows you to maintain things thrilling.

Be Brief

The term "small speak" was coined for a motive, so it is vital to maintain your story to a minimum. If your narrative takes you extra than a minute to complete, it is probably that it's a chunk too lengthy-winded.

You is probably worried that presenting a concise story will result in even more awkward silence. Remember that you're having a dialogue, not a overall performance for the gain of others. You do not want to take over the conversation and never allow the alternative character a hazard to respond on your points of view.

In small communicate, you're now not predicted to enter your private thoughts, emotions, and aims; rather, it's supposed to be a pleasantry. However, there is no denying that it is able to additionally lead to some as a substitute banal testimonies being stated whilst status in a protracted line or throughout a clumsy creation.

A Few Storytelling Tips:

Taking the entirety we've just discussed into attention, right here are a few techniques that will help you put together in telling your subsequent story.